The Song Tradition
of Tristan da Cunha

INDIANA UNIVERSITY FOLKLORE INSTITUTE
MONOGRAPH SERIES, VOL. 22

Bloomington, 1970

Peter A. Munch

The Song Tradition
of Tristan da Cunha

Published by
INDIANA UNIVERSITY RESEARCH CENTER
FOR THE LANGUAGE SCIENCES, BLOOMINGTON
Mouton & Co., The Hague, The Netherlands

The Indiana University Folklore Series was founded in 1939
for the publication of occasional papers and monographs.

Orders for the U.S.A. and Canada should be
placed with Humanities Press, Inc., 303
Park Avenue South, New York, N.Y. 10010

Orders from all other countries should be sent to
Mouton & Company, Publishers, The Hague, The Netherlands.

Printed in the United States of America

PREFACE

The plans for the Norwegian Scientific Expedition to Tristan da Cunha 1937-1938 included a medical, a dental, and a sociological survey of the island community. Collection of folklore material, specifically folk songs and dances, was not originally considered. However, it soon became evident that song and dance played a very prominent part in the lives of these highly gregarious people. Their popular songs and dances, therefore, could not fail to attract our attention. Besides, they proved to be valuable material in the study of the cultural impulses received by this island community in the past.

Although an amateur in the field of balladry and folklore, I therefore set out to record some of the songs and dance tunes. No recording equipment was available, and only a limited time could be devoted to the task. However, with the help of some of the more literate Islanders, I managed to put down on paper some fifty songs and ditties and about twenty of the more frequently used dance tunes played on the accordion or on the fiddle. It is regrettable that time and preparations did not permit a more extensive recording of dances as well as of dance tunes and songs. But no one knew at the time of our visit that we were witnessing the last days, as it were, of a cultural tradition relatively untouched by the technology of the twentieth century.

Later developments have drastically changed the situation of Tristan da Cunha. An overwhelming world civilization, based on a superior technology and electronic mass communication, has reached out even to this remote spot in the middle of the ocean and has drawn it under its uniforming influence, depriving the community of much of its cultural autonomy. Among the things that had to yield was the song tradition. As one could predict, and as was confirmed by a renewed visit to Tristan da Cunha by the author in 1964-65, the old song tradition has been drowned out by the radio, the phonograph, and the tape recorder.

All this has of course lent additional interest to the small collection of traditional songs and dance tunes that I was able to bring with me from our four months' stay on Tristan da Cunha in 1938. They are presented here with little or no reference to later developments. However, on the basis of more recent observations among the Tristan Islanders, both in England during their short exile after the volcanic eruption of 1961, and on Tristan after their return — and this time with the aid of a tape recorder — an epilogue has been added to bring the account of the song tradition of Tristan da Cunha up to date.

Of the number of Tristan Islanders who contributed generously to this collection of songs and dance tunes, special thanks are due to Mrs. Agnes Rogers, who wrote down a number of song texts obtained from other women, particularly from the late Mrs. Lily Green, and to Mrs. Alice Glass (at that time, Miss Swain), our excellent cook and housekeeper, who patiently assisted me in transcribing some of the tunes. Also the late Mrs. Frances Repetto, who died in an influenza epidemic in 1948, gave valuable assistance by writing down the texts of some of her own songs. My most cordial gratitude goes to Mr. and Mrs. Fred Swain and Mary Swain for warm hospitality and generous assistance during both of my visits to Tristan da Cunha.

Thanks are also due to Professor Fred Denker, of the Department of Music, Southern Illinois University, who was kind enough to read through an early draft of the manuscript and offered valuable suggestions and advice. He is, of course, in no way responsible for remaining errors and shortcomings.

The Norwegian Scientific Expedition to Tristan da Cunha, 1937-1938, which made this collection of songs and dance tunes possible, was planned, organized, and directed by Dr. Erling Christophersen, formerly of the Botanical Museum, University of Oslo, Norway. Generous financial support was given by Mr. Lars Christensen, Sandefjord, Norway, and by the following scientific foundations in Norway: Det Videnskapelige Forskningsfond av 1919, Fridtjof Nansens Fond, and Norsk Varekrigsforsikrings Fond.

Sociological field research among the Tristan Islanders at Calshot, England, was conducted by the author during the summer of 1962 under a grant from the Social Science Research Council. Further investigations on the island of Tristan da Cunha October 1964 to May 1965, were sponsored by the National Science Foundation and Southern Illinois University.

Carbondale, Illinois

Peter A. Munch

CONTENTS

INTRODUCTION

1. The Community

One of the most isolated spots ever inhabited by man is without doubt the little island of Tristan da Cunha. With less than forty square miles of land area, the island is only a speck in the vast expanse of the South Atlantic Ocean, separated from the nearest inhabited place by some 1,500 miles of open sea. And, from the hand of Nature, a most inhospitable place it is, windswept and rugged, nothing but a huge volcanic cone reaching to a height of more than 6,000 feet above sea level, with the stormy South Atlantic beating against its shores. Yet on this island lives a small community of about 260 people who have won the reputation of being among the most hospitable, friendly, and cheerful people in the world.

At the time of its discovery in 1506, Tristan da Cunha, with its two smaller satellite islands, Inaccessible and Nightingale, was the undisturbed home of a great number of fur seals, sea elephants, and sea birds, besides a few peculiar species of flightless land birds and some small reptiles. Adventurous man, attracted primarily by the fur seal, made a few attempts at colonization, the most famous of which was that of a certain Jonathan Lambert, of Salem, Massachusetts, who, in February 1811, issued a manifesto to the world announcing himself the sole proprietor of Tristan da Cunha and inviting ships of all nations to call at his place for provisions. His idea was to make Tristan da Cunha a "refreshment station" for sailing ships, where they could conveniently call for fresh provisions of water, meat, and vegetables, and occasionally pick up a cargo of seal skins. But Lambert soon after perished at sea, and it was not until 1816 that a permanent settlement was formed. In that year the island was formally annexed by the British and furnished with a small garrison of about forty men, most of them "Hottentots" from the Cape Colony. The party, which was accompanied by some ten women, mostly wives of the officers, settled on the northwestern foreland where the settlement has remained ever since, with the rank and file "Hottentots" camping on the other side of a ravine still known as Hottentot Gulch.

The garrison was abandoned the following year. But three of its members, a Scottish corporal of the artillery and two English masons, decided to remain, apparently in an attempt to establish a utopian community based on the principles of communal ownership and absolute equality. William Glass, the Scot, who was the leader of the party, was accompanied by his wife, described as a "Cape Creole," of Dutch origin. The three men were soon joined by others — sailors of various

European backgrounds but mostly British, and with a good admixture of American whalers from New England. In 1827, five or six women of mixed racial stock were brought from St. Helena in an American sloop.[1]

The establishment of a permanent settlement on Tristan da Cunha coincided with – and was partly made possible by – a notable increase in transoceanic sailing traffic, which probably reached its peak during the first half of the nineteenth century. It is important to note that the island is situated in the so-called West Wind Belt, or "Antitrades," which formed the natural and preferred traffic lane for sailing vessels en route from Europe or North America to the Cape and points east. Consequently, in the early days of the settlement, there was a lively traffic of sailing vessels of various descriptions in the surrounding waters, and Jonathan Lambert's idea of making Tristan da Cunha a refreshment station for sailing ships was not at all far fetched. Although he did not live to carry out his plan, his idea did not die with him, and it became even more feasible when the sealing and whaling traffic in the adjacent waters took on considerable proportions.

The abundance of seal and sea elephant attracted English sealers as early as 1812, and their numbers increased during the following decades. A few place names still in use on Tristan are reminiscent of this traffic, such as Seal Bay, Elephant Bay, Bull Point, Trypot, and Tommy's Ile'ous (contracted from "oil house"). And from the 1820s onward, the waters around Tristan da Cunha became a regular hunting ground for New England whalers, mostly from New Bedford, New London, and Salem. In consequence, trade with passing ships became in fact an important and profitable occupation for the Tristan Islanders for some time.

There are no records of the number of ships that called at Tristan da Cunha during the early years of the settlement. But there is reason to believe that the number was considerable and provided a steady contact between the island and the world outside. One indication of the amount of traffic in the immediate vicinity of Tristan is the number of shipwrecks that occurred there. Twenty or more total shipwrecks have been recorded which took place at Tristan da Cunha and the neighboring islands during the period 1817-1898, all of them involving sailing ships. Six of them occurred in the 1870s and four during the 1890s.[2] The whaling traffic seems to have reached its peak around 1840. But even in 1851, it was reported that as many as thirty-five ships called at the island during that year. In 1852, there were twenty-six calls. And as late as 1876, Captain Brine, of H.M.S. *Wolverene,* was informed that "latterly not less than an annual average of 20 ships have called off the settlement for provisions and water."[3]

During the following years, however, these conditions changed drastically. In the first place, from around 1880, there was a sharp decline in the whaling traffic as seals, sea elephants, and whales were practically exterminated from the shores of Tristan and from the surrounding waters. In 1886, only ten years after Captain Brine's visit, an official report stated that "the trade which they used to carry on with passing ships and with whalers no longer exists, as the whalers have almost

Tristan da Cunha

Peter Green's House
Built About 1840
Occupied 1938 by Frances Repetto
and her son, Chief Willie Repetto

ceased to call." It was noted that during the twelve months, August 1885 - July 1886, only two whalers had communicated with the island.[4] Throughout the ten years, 1904 - 1913, according to a register kept on the island, no more than thirteen American whalers touched at Tristan, and after that time they disappeared completely. But also the transports vanished as the transoceanic traffic was taken over by steamships which followed a new and more direct course, independent of the trade winds. Besides, the Suez Canal, which was opened in 1869, diverted much of the Far-Eastern traffic entirely away from the South Atlantic. Today, none of the main trade routes passes within a distance of 1300 miles from Tristan da Cunha. The island community, which formerly had an important part to play in the world's household, found itself in almost complete isolation.

This is the background upon which we must see the cultural tradition of the Tristan community. Since most of the settlers were British, it is only to be expected that the British influence has remained predominant. The spoken language is a dialect of English, and most of the folklore, including the songs, obviously came ultimately from the same source. The remarkable influence of William Glass, the founder of the community, must account for a definite Scottish strain, as seen, for instance, in the style and architecture of the houses. A slight Boer influence was seen in the dress of the little girls, particularly their headdress (kappie), and in certain Dutch-African loanwords. But the strongest influence besides the British was evidently received from American whalers, as is particularly apparent in the boat building and, as we shall see, in certain parts of the song tradition.

Whatever their ultimate source, however, the various cultural impulses obviously came to the Tristan community through the pelagic traditions of the sailing ships. Although the original settlers, William Glass and his two companions, would probably be described as "landlubbers," practically all of the later settlers were sailors or otherwise roamers of the sea. And through the years, all the contacts that the Islanders had with the world outside were of course effected through the media of ships and sailors. In fact, from its earliest years, the little community on Tristan da Cunha was itself part and parcel of that distinct and peculiar way of life which we may describe as the heritage of the seven seas, and which, although founded on British Navy traditions, was international in flavor and cosmopolitan in outlook.

While this tradition has all but vanished from the decks and bulkheads of the modern, fast moving tankers and freighters, the definitely "salty" stamp of the Tristan community was preserved, apparently through the effects of an increasing isolation. In later years, at least up to the time of the Second World War, one of the most outstanding and conspicuous traits of the Tristan community has been an extreme conservatism, with an almost deferential attitude toward tradition. Actually, up to the war, the Tristan community exhibited many forms of culture that seemed to belong in the nineteenth century. In 1938, we met this conservative disposition of the Islanders in all aspects of life, in social organization and institutions no less than in costume. And these traditional forms of life were often rigidly adhered to, like a bulwark against change and cultural decay. In fact, these old. forms of culture and social life had achieved a kind of supremacy over any new forms that might be introduced, and caused a firm, though unconscious, resistance to be put up against any innovation from outside, as witnessed by a few frustrated attempts to introduce new and improved techniques of agriculture. The Tristan Islanders, therefore, have generally made a peculiar impression on visitors; there is something old fashioned about them. Apparently, as the community grew more and more isolated, the absence of a constant flow of impulses from outside caused the process of cultural change – present to some degree in every human community – to slow down to the extent that the community of Tristan da Cunha really became one of the last living relics of the days of the sailing ships.

2. The Social Setting

It did not take long for the members of our expedition to discover that these rock-bound mariners really did live up to their reputation of being extremely friendly, cheerful, and gregarious people. They were of a sensitive, almost sentimental disposition, and easily gave vent to feelings of sorrow as well as of joy. Their sympathies were strong and real, and their sociability was pronounced. Although the original principles of communal work and ownership were long since forgotten, it soon became evident that celebrations and gregarious gatherings played a prominent part in their lives in work as well as in leisure. And wherever they gathered in groups, dance and song were natural and cherished forms of expression.

On the least occasion, it was customary to have a dance "for the whole island" in the "school house" which, in fact, was built mainly for this purpose – a long, roughly constructed stone building in the center of the village, next to the church, in the usual style with a thatched roof, but with a wooden floor of solid planks that looked as if they had been procured from a shipwreck. The old ship's bell, rescued from the shipwrecked *Mabel Clark* in 1878 and subsequently mounted on the gable of the church, had an important function besides serving as a church bell: when rung in the evening after supper, it was usually a call for a communal dance in the school house. And it happened quite frequently.

There were, in the first place, the perennial communal festivals, the most important of which were Christmas and Easter. Christmas was usually celebrated with dance and merrymaking every night from Boxing Day till New Year's Eve, and on New Year's night the Islanders would go "Christmas guisers," as they still would call the mummers in Scottish fashion, going from house to house till break of day, with dance and song in each house as they went along. Also, Easter was an occasion for a communal dance or two, and even Shrove Tuesday was celebrated with a dance in keeping with old English tradition. An occasion which naturally called for a communal dance was the visit of a ship, especially if the ship happened to stay overnight.

In addition to these communal festivals, there were various opportunities for individuals to put on a feast. Certain family celebrations usually followed a set pattern: there would be a mid-day dinner for "relations" in the house, followed by an open house for tea in the afternoon and a dance for "all hands" in the school house at night. The most important family milestones celebrated in this manner were weddings and certain birthdays. On a child's first birthday, it was almost mandatory for the parents to give a dance. Even more important was the twenty-first birthday, when godparents would pressure the parents to put on a big feast and even help prepare it with great extravagance — at the parents' expense. Likewise, when a man reached fifty, he was expected to give a dance for the whole island, and a prominent man like "Chief" Willie Repetto, who had been appointed Chief Man by one of the resident ministers but otherwise had no more authority than anybody else, could even mark his thirty-sixth birthday with a dance for "all hands." Besides, the Islanders would have small, private, more informal dances in their houses whenever they felt like it.

On these occasions, whether private or communal, there would usually be a long pause in the dancing some time during the evening while the fiddler or accordion player "took a spell." At this time, one or another of the Islanders would get up and sing a song for entertainment — always after a ritual of proper prodding and persuasion and repeated assurances from the singer that "I don't know no songs." In the case of a privately sponsored dance, it was first of all the duty of the host to provide this kind of entertainment, either in person or by proxy, and it properly went as an accompaniment to the tea and "biscuits" served by the hostess. But after the host had given his piece, others could be persuaded to perform as well.

The gregariousness of the Tristan Islanders was also expressed in much of their work. As is common in relatively undifferentiated "folk" societies, the Islanders had developed certain rather firmly established patterns of life in which particular kinds of work were inseparably associated with certain specific forms of gregarious entertainment and recreation.[5] They liked to work in gangs, and especially if the work was of a seasonal or occasional nature, such as an apple harvest, egg gathering, or building a house or a boat, there was generally a strong inclination to turn it into a festive occasion.[6] If the work was performed near the settlement, the wives would take turns to dress up in their Sunday best and bring some extra treat to the workers for lunch. And when the day's work was done, there would be a meal for the whole gang, followed by an evening of mutual entertainment with songs and perhaps a dance.

A particularly cherished form of recreational work was "going 'round the beaches." To every Islander, the mere words used to bring about pleasant memories of trips, on foot or by boat, to the other side of the island, Stony Beach, Seal Bay, or Sandy Point, or even "over there" to Nightingale, always with an agreeable mixture of work and play, spending the night in caves or in primitive huts away from the routine of everyday life. The Islanders never go on such trips without a task of some kind: there are cattle to be looked after, there are penguin rookeries with eggs and feathers to be picked, and there are orchards and berries. But it is as if the work itself gets a stamp of the holiday spirit that prevails on these excursions. Women often take part, mostly to assist the men in their work, but sometimes just to have a trip and a change from the daily routine – they even put on nice clothes for the occasion. And at night there would be songs around a blazing bonfire under a starlit sky.

 Not everybody was expected to be able to sing a song on a given occasion, and some naturally had a reputation of being better singers than others. But the performance of songs was not limited to a few more or less "professional" singers. In mixed gatherings, the men would dominate the singing – in fact, I never heard a woman perform a song "in public." But in the "carding gang," where women would get together to card and spin wool, or in the family circle, the women would also sing.

 As is generally the case in Anglo-American song tradition, the songs were always performed solo, and with no instrumental accompaniment.[7] Occasionally, in some of the songs, there would be a unison chorus. Otherwise, group singing never occurred except in church, where the unaccompanied hymns were sung with great fervor. There is obviously a connection between this preference for the solo song and the strong sense of proprietorship associated with most of the songs. Generally, a song was attached to a particular singer and was regarded as "his" song to the extent that it would have been considered highly inappropriate for anyone else to perform the song, at least in his presence. For this reason, although one man boasted that he knew "hundreds of songs," the repertoire of each singer could be quite limited, sometimes perhaps to just one song. This, of course, does not mean that he might not know a great number of songs; it only means that the number of songs that were "his" and that he might be expected to perform was limited. This may in fact be regarded as a primitive form of copyright, enforced – like any other social code in this island community – by a spontaneous and almost invisible social control, whose most important sanction is a loss of respect and prestige for the transgressor.[8]

 On the other hand, a song might "belong" to more than one singer, then often in different versions, each singer claiming, of course, that his version was really the authentic one.

 According to this social code, anyone could pick up a song from an outside source and make it his own. This is in fact how all the songs of Tristan da Cunha have been acquired in the past as there were no original songs endemic to the island. Occasionally, this might still happen, as in the case of a version of Weatherly's

"Danny Boy," which was sung to me by Alice Swain (now Mrs. Glass). She had learned the text from a song book and picked up the tune from a phonograph record. However, with the increasing isolation of the community, this became a rare occurrence. The normal way of "acquiring" a song was by "inheritance," and – as seems to be the usual pattern in the Anglo-American song tradition – the regular line of transmission was the kinship line: songs were learned and taken over mostly from parents, grandparents, uncles, or aunts.

3. Kinship Lines of Transmission

There were in particular, two kinship lines, frequently intermarried, that appeared to be the main carriers of the song tradition on Tristan da Cunha, although it was by no means limited to them. Obviously, in collecting the song texts and tunes presented in the following pages, I was directed to those Islanders who knew the greatest number of songs, or who had a reputation of being good singers or frequent performers, and it is surely not a mere accident when it was afterwards found that of the fourteen informants who contributed to the collection, thirteen belonged to one or the other of these two kinship lines, with some of the most generous contributors having their roots in both (see Chart 1).

One of these kinship lines stems from Thomas Swain, a British sailor with an adventurous career, who wound up as one of the early settlers of Tristan da Cunha. He had served under Lord Nelson, and island tradition had him identified with that very sailor who is said to have caught Nelson in his arms as the Admiral fell mortally wounded on the deck of the *Victory*.[9] Swain's service under Nelson, however, was not in the *Victory* but in the *Theseus*. After having served eighteen years in the British Navy, he ran away, was taken prisoner by the French and, "to his sad disgrace as a British sailor," was induced to serve with them against his native country. After three years in the French service, he was recaptured by the British and remained for nine years a French prisoner in England, "not daring for his life to own the truth."[10] After the end of the Napoleonic War, he went to sea in a merchantman and, in 1826, was induced to join the little utopia on Tristan da Cunha, at that time comprising no more than eight adult members. Swain was then fifty-two years old. The following year he married one of the colored women brought from St. Helena.

Thomas Swain had ten children, three sons and seven daughters. Four of his daughters remained on Tristan all their lives. The others went away. But two of his sons came back to resettle on Tristan. They were Thomas Hill Swain and his younger brother, Samuel R. Swain. Both of them had been away in sailing ships for shorter or longer periods between 1850 and 1870. The older one, who had married a Tristan girl, had even taken his family to Cape Town and made his home there for ten years

Chart 1. THE PRINCIPAL KINSHIP LINES OF SONG TRADITION

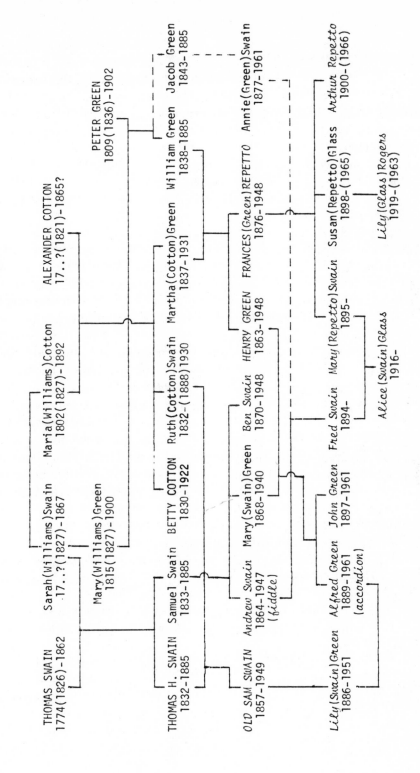

Main links capitalized. Names of *informants in script.*

Years in parenthesis indicate dates of arrival to, or departure from, Tristan da Cunha.

before returning to Tristan in 1870. Samuel married a girl from St. Helena, and both brothers eventually settled down on the island but, in 1885, perished at sea with thirteen other men in the worst disaster that ever happened to the community. A lifeboat, carrying no less than two-thirds of the grown men on the island, set out to board a passing ship, then disappeared without a trace.

After the lifeboat accident, there was a general exodus from Tristan da Cunha, mostly of widows and their families. During the next fifteen years about sixty persons left the island, reducing the population to half its former size. Most of the migrants went to South Africa or to New England, where many of them had relatives from earlier emigrations.

Of Thomas Hill Swain's nine children, only one remained on Tristan.   That was Old Sam Swain, who always went by that name, partly to distinguish him from his younger cousin, "Little" Sam Swain, partly because, when old Peter Green died in 1902, Old Sam, at the age of forty-five, really became the oldest man on the island. Born in 1857, he was eighty at the time of our visit. With his flowing white beard, he looked like a patriarch. But he carried his age with an agility that is characteristic of these very healthy people.

Old Sam Swain was one of the more popular singers in the community, and it is obvious that he had learned many of his songs from his father. He sometimes described them as stemming "from the shipping days of Thomas Hill Swain." To judge from Old Sam's role as a singer and from the number of songs known by him and his daughter, Lily Green, Thomas Hill Swain seems to have been a rich source.

Thomas Hill's younger brother, Samuel R. Swain, may have been one of the main sources for the tradition of instrumental music on Tristan since both of the chief musicians of the island at the time of our visit were his direct descendants. Andrew Swain, the fiddler, was his son, and the accordion player, Alfred Green (Lily Green's husband), was his grandson. But there were songs in that branch of the family, too. Ben Swain, Andrew's younger brother, who remained a bachelor all his life, was a relatively frequent performer at the communal dances. He seemed to have the memory of quite a number of songs that he had learned either from his father or from his uncle, although he was a man of modest intelligence and sometimes got his songs mixed up.

The other important kinship line of song tradition on Tristan is traceable to a Dutchman, Pieter Willem Groen. He arrived in 1836 in the American schooner *Emily*. She had been hunting seal and sea elephant on the south side of the island but was driven ashore in a sudden gale and wrecked. All hands were saved, and three of the crew decided to stay, Pieter Groen being one of them. He changed his name to Peter William Green, married one of the St. Helena girls (a daughter of Thomas Swain's wife), and remained on the island till his death in 1902.

Peter Green was twenty-seven years old when he was cast ashore on Tristan. Little is known of his past except that he was born in 1809 at Katwijk, Holland.

Old Sam Swain
in 1938

Henry Green
in 1938

Apparently, as quite a young lad, he went to sea, and in September 1835, he shipped out from New York in the schooner that eventually brought him to Tristan. He never left the island again and was to become a prominent person in the little community. After the death of William Glass, in 1853, he eventually became the undisputed leader, although, unlike Glass, he was never explicitly appointed head man. His was a typical "charismatic" leadership. He simply acted on behalf of the Islanders and, being probably more literate than most, carried on a correspondence with the Admiralty and other British authorities who, in fact, regarded him as the unofficial "Governor" of Tristan da Cunha.

As a resident of Tristan, Peter Green outlived all of his eight children. His youngest son died as the result of an accident on board a sailing ship, and the remaining three sons were in the lifeboat that disappeared in 1885. On that occasion, he also lost a son-in-law and three grandsons. Three of his daughters had been married out of Tristan before that time — two of them were living in Cape Town — and the fourth daughter, now a widow with three small children, soon after left to join her sisters. Even most of his grandchildren went away, partly with their widowed mothers, partly on their own. In the end, out of some thirty or more grandchildren of Peter Green's born on Tristan, only four remained on the island.

In spite of this, the Green tradition remained a strong influence on Tristan da Cunha. After the old man's death, leadership seems to have been more or less thrust upon his grandson, Henry Green, but was soon taken over by Henry's younger sister, Frances, and her husband, Andrea Repetto, an Italian sailor who arrived in 1892, when the sailing. ship *Italia* caught fire off Tristan and was run ashore at Stony Beach. After her husband died in 1911, Frances Repetto soon became such a powerful influence that it was natural for visitors to describe her as the "Queen" of Tristan da Cunha, although to the Islanders she was just "Fannie."

Frances Repetto was indeed a remarkable person. She was born in 1876 as the youngest child of Peter Green's eldest and apparently most prominent son, William Green. Her mother, who lived to be ninety-four, also seems to have been an important and respected person in the community; she was a daughter of Alexander Cotton, another early settler of outstanding influence. However, when Frances was only nine years old, the lifeboat disaster swept away nearly all of her male relatives. On that occasion, she lost her father, three brothers, and eight uncles, and the only male relative she had left, besides her grandfather and a three-year-old cousin, was her thirteen-years' older brother, Henry Green. In 1894, before she was eighteen, she was married to Andrea Repetto. At thirty-five, she was a widow with seven children, the eldest being a girl of fifteen, and the youngest, a boy of two.

By all who met her, Frances Repetto was known as an exceptional and outstanding personality. She was quite intelligent and expressed herself well. Although she had never been away from the island of her birth, her conversation disclosed considerable wisdom and knowledge of human nature and an amazingly

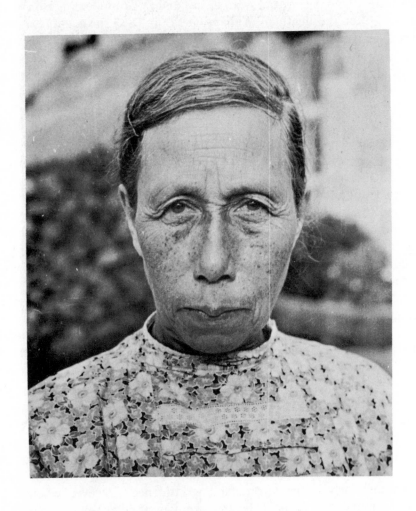

Frances Repetto
in 1938

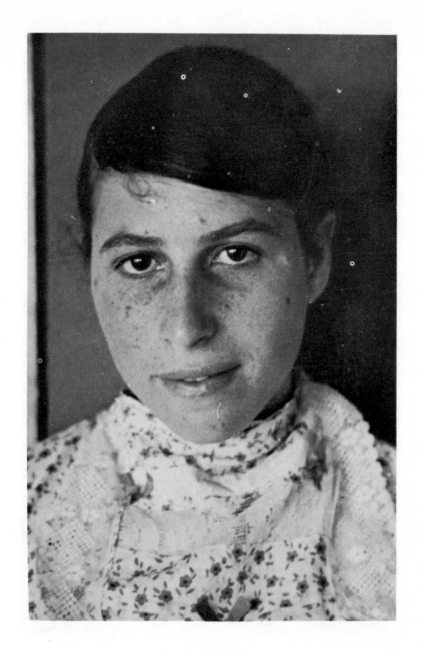

Alice Swain
in 1938

Fred Swain
in 1938

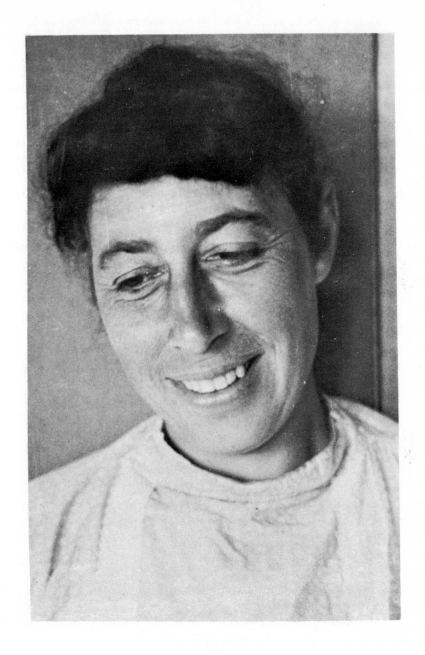

Mary Swain
in 1938

broad outlook. Her sense of justice was strong, and she held very definite opinions, well supported and frankly expressed, of what she considered right and proper. She is reported to have been a strict and consistent upbringer of her children, and toward her own grandchildren she showed that kindly firmness which leaves no room for a compromise. Evidence of her strong personality is the fact that her family remained very close, socially speaking, even in later years, forming a well integrated joint-family under matriarchal rule. At the same time, she was a warmhearted woman, kind and cheerful, and loved with reverence by all. Her death in an influenza epidemic in 1948 was not only a sorrowful blow to the whole community of Tristan da Cunha, it attracted the attention of the world press.

It was quite apparent that both Henry Green and Frances Repetto were important links in the song tradition of Tristan da Cunha. Both of them evidently knew a great number of songs, and Henry Green was a frequent performer. Also in this case, the transmission of the songs was mainly in the kinship line although, for obvious reasons, it had, as it were, jumped a generation. Peter Green, the grandfather, was the one who was most frequently mentioned as the model and source. And a strong and positive attitude toward this tradition was maintained in the following generations, particularly among Frances Repetto's children and grandchildren.

One of these grandchildren of Frances Repetto's was Alice Swain (whose married name is Glass), our cook and general help in the house that we erected for our headquarters. She, too, like her grandmother and her mother, is quite intelligent, and she turned out to be my best informant on island custom and usage as well as on songs. She seemed to know well every song on the island, and she proved a great help to me, particularly in my effort to transcribe the tunes.

Alice Swain had song tradition on both sides of her family, although — with Frances Repetto being her maternal grandmother — she was more attached to her mother's family and its traditions. Her father is Fred Swain, the eldest son of Andrew Swain, the fiddler. He is a retiring sort of person who needed more than the usual prodding before he would sing. His best performance was in the family circle, and it was there, in the fairly large kitchen of his house, in the dim light of a dying fire, that I picked up some of his songs.

Fred Swain himself had connections with the Green clan. His mother was a granddaughter of Peter Green and a cousin of Henry Green and Frances Repetto. However, there happened to be a considerable social distance between these two branches of the Green clan. Contributing to this may have been the fact that Fred Swain's grandfather, Jacob Green, as well as his uncle, Charles Green, had married into the rivalling Glass-Hagan coalition of clans.[11] And in those clans, singing did not seem to be a part of the cherished family tradition.

There were even other ties of marriage between the Swains and the Greens, which may have served to reinforce the singing tradition in these clans. Of the greatest importance for the perpetuation of such a tradition in these particular kinship lines was probably the fact that they were closely aligned and multifariously related by marriage already in the first and second generations. We have already heard that a daughter of Thomas Swain's wife was married to Peter Green, who on that basis recognized the much younger Thomas Hill Swain as his brother-in-law, a relationship which implied a very strong social bond on Tristan, at least in later years.[12] Still more important for a continuity in the common family tradition was probably the fact that both families were allied by marriage with the Cotton family.

Alexander Cotton, sometimes called by his Navy *nom de guerre*, John Taylor, was another early settler with a colorful past in the British Navy. He has been described as "a thorough old man-of-war's man" who "had been in much active service during the [Napoleonic] war . . . had seen some fighting, and, of course, had learnt to worship Nelson," of whom he remained "a devout admirer" the rest of his life.[13] He and a shipmate had visited Tristan a couple of times while the British garrison was still there, and once after the garrison had left; and so delighted were they with the community and its egalitarian principles that they decided to join it as settlers. They went home to England, were paid off, and, after having spent all their money, asked the Admiralty to give them a free passage to the island, offering to give up all claims to a pension in return. Their humble request was granted, and soon they were landed on Tristan da Cunha from the brig-of-war *Satellite*, bound for India.

This was in 1821, when the community was only four years old and there were no more than half a dozen men on the island, William Glass still being the only one with a family. Cotton remained there for the rest of his life.

Apparently no one could challenge William Glass' leadership in this community during his lifetime. Nevertheless, Alexander Cotton soon acquired a prominent position among the settlers. In this practically seaborne community, he had the advantage over Glass, the artilleryman, of being an experienced sailor. He seems to have put himself in charge of the boats, and as early as 1824 he was described as one of the leaders.[14] He and Thomas Swain, the other Navy man who arrived five years later, were among the five men who in 1827 made a bargain with an American skipper to have five women brought from St. Helena. Sarah and Maria Williams, the two chosen by Swain and Cotton, were sisters.

When Peter Green arrived in 1836, he appears to have joined this little band of sailors. We have already mentioned that he married a daughter of Sarah Williams, who had married Thomas Swain.[15] And the relationship was strongly reinforced in the next generation. Three of Peter Green's four sons eventually married daughters of Alexander Cotton; and when a fourth daughter of Cotton was married to Thomas Hill Swain, an intricate network of socially recognized and significant relationships was established between the three families.[16]

Of Alexander Cotton's twelve children, two died young. Two sons and four sons-in-law (among them Thomas Hill Swain and William and Jeremiah Green) were

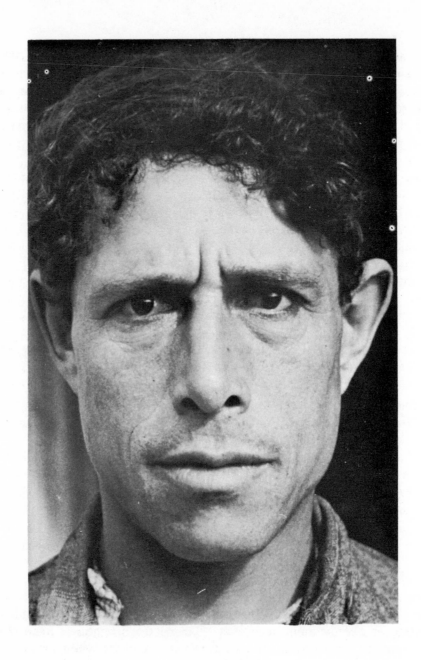

Arthur Repetto
in 1938

lost in the lifeboat in 1885, and the ensuing wave of emigrations left only two daughters remaining on Tristan. But there is reason to believe that these two women became important retainers and transmitters of island tradition, the more important because for quite some time they appear to have been the only living links to the past in a generation that was practically wiped out by the lifeboat disaster and the emigrations that followed. Both of them lived to a ripe old age, and both were described as prominent and highly respected persons in the community.

The two women were Betty Cotton, Alexander Cotton's eldest daughter, who remained unmarried and died in 1922 at the age of ninety-two, and Martha Green, the mother of Henry Green and Frances Repetto, who was ninety-four when she died in 1931. Betty Cotton, in particular, seems to have been a presonification of island tradition and an inexhaustible source of yarns and tales, her personal memory covering some eighty years of island history. For the song tradition on Tristan da Cunha it must have been of some importance that these two women formed a long-lasting living link between the Swain, Cotton, and Green lines of family tradition. It is certainly of significance to note that the three principal links of song tradition in the third generation, Old Sam Swain, Henry Green, and Frances Repetto, all had Betty Cotton for an aunt. Although she was never referred to explicitly as the source of any particular song, she may well have served as a reinforcer of the song tradition in both the Swain and the Green kinship lines.

This remarkable concentration of the song tradition in certain lineages of the Swain and Green clans does not imply, of course, that only members of these were singers, nor does it mean that most of the songs were referable to Thomas Swain, Alexander Cotton, or Peter Green as their sources. It does mean, however, that these kinship lines were the carriers of a tradition that attached a particular positive value to the performance of songs as a form of entertainment, whereby they jointly functioned as a reinforcer of the song tradition in the community as a whole.

4. The Sources

Nearly all the songs current on Tristan da Cunha in 1938 were traditional in the sense that they had been transmitted from one generation to another without the aid of writing or phonographic recording. "Danny Boy" appeared to be the only exception. And, as we have already noted, not one of these songs was endemic to Tristan. Obviously, the songs had been brought there by roamers of the sea, whether they were settlers, natives of the island, or just visitors.

From the variety of songs contained in the small collection from Tristan da Cunha presented here, one gets an impression of the kind of cultural baggage that the motley crowd of seafarers brought to the island. There were epical ballads, some of them with a long ancestral line leading all the way back to the classical ballads of

Scotland and England, such as "The Golden Vanity," "The Butcher Boy," and the never-dying "Barbara Allen." There were sailor songs, both lively shanties and lyrical, sometimes sentimental, pieces about true and false love, or about mothers and sweethearts waiting for the sailor boy who died at sea, but also dramatic tales about heroic deeds and courage shown by the little boy or girl where strong men failed. There were whaling songs, drinking songs, and humorous parodies and ditties. Finally, one could find American "blackface" minstrels as well as variations of some of the most popular romantic minstrel songs of the late nineteenth century, such as Nolan's "Little Annie Rooney," Benny Hanby's "Darling Nelly Gray," Henry Work's "The Ship that Never Returned," and, as already mentioned, Weatherly's heart-wrenching "Danny Boy."

The ultimate origin of the songs, even of the newer ones, was, of course, long lost in the process of oral transmission and was, as in most folk tradition, not a matter of concern. Nor did the singers seem to care about knowing the sources by which the songs had been brought to Tristan. The older singers would sometimes refer to the "old hands" in general, more infrequently to specific individuals of the preceding generation, as the sources of some of their songs. But already the next generation did not seem to be concerned about origins. These songs were taken for granted as an integral part of their cultural heritage, and no one seemed to care where they came from or who brought them.

With regard to the question of origin, it is well to keep in mind that Tristan da Cunha was situated in one of the main traffic lanes for sailing vessels bound to South Africa and the Far East, and that throughout the greater part of the nineteenth century there was a considerable traffic of "transports" of various descriptions. It is true that visiting sailors seldom stayed long enough to make a lasting contribution to the song tradition of the island, although an experienced folk singer may pick up a song with amazing quickness. However, the relatively frequent calls of sailing vessels at Tristan gave an opportunity for young men of the island to ship out and roam the sea, and many were those who availed themselves of it. Although most of them probably disappeared for ever, many of them did return for occasional visits, sometimes for periods of several years, and a few of them, like Thomas Swain's two sons, came back for permanent settlement. These sailors of Tristan certainly brought with them new impulses and new knowledge which served generally to reinforce the pelagic heritage of this island community. That there were songs among the treasures brought back to Tristan in this way can hardly be doubted and was confirmed in several instances.

Besides, there were numerous shipwrecks, when sometimes several months might pass before the survivors were picked up by another vessel touching at the island. There is good reason to believe that these shipwrecks made important contributions to the cultural heritage of Tristan da Cunha, besides furnishing much needed woodwork for houses and boats, and an occasional settler. At least one song, which became very popular on Tristan, both as a song and as a dance tune played on the accordion, is known positively to have been brought by a shipwreck: "Little Annie Rooney"(p. 98) was introduced by a sailor on board the *Allen Shaw,* a sailing ship that was wrecked at the island in 1893.[17] Another song, the blackface minstrel "Josiphus Orange Blossom"or "Happy Darkey" (p. 109) was reported to have come to Tristan with the *Mabel Clark,* the American vessel that suffered a similar fate in 1878.

Born as the Tristan community was of the heritage of the seven seas, and with the umbilical cord unbroken for so long, it is self-evident that the song tradition of the community should be dominated by the characteristic sailor song. The unmistakable stamp of British tradition carried by many of these songs is also to be expected. Not only were most of the settlers British; it is well known, too, that the cultural heritage of the seven seas, which flourished under the bulging canvas and in the gloomy forecastles of the sailing ships and spread to every seaport in the world, had an important foundation in British Navy traditions and was carried mainly by an overwhelmingly numerous British merchant marine. We are, however, reminded of the truly global and polyglot nature of this heritage when we consider the fact that many of the songs of this tradition were in circulation in many tongues.

It may be of interest in this connection to note that at least three of the most typical sailor songs recorded on Tristan da Cunha, "Her Sailor Boy" (p. 51) "A Light in the Window" (p. 60), and the tearful farewell song which we have rendered here under the title "The Sailor Boy" (p. 58), have close parallels in the Norwegian language. How very close these parallels could stay, even under the hazards of translation and oral transmission, is demonstrated by the text of a Norwegian traditional sailor song, *For syv aar siden* ("Seven Years Ago"), as compared with the three Tristan versions of the corresponding British favorite, "Her Sailor Boy":[18]

For syv aar siden

1. En pige vandred udi en have,
   til hende kom der en ung sjømand:
   "Sig, hvorfor sidder du her allene?
   Giv mig dit hjerte, giv mig din hand." (A,B,C: 1)

2. "Paa saadan tale jeg ei kan svare,
   thi jeg er født udav ringe stand;
   din tjenerinde det kan jeg vaere,
   men aldrig, aldrig du blir min mand." (B,C: 2)

3. "Min tjenerinde du ei skal vaere,
   jeg har i sandhed respekt for dig.

Nei du maa blive min hjertenskjaere,
for jeg har guld nok til dig og mig." (B,C:3)

4. "Jeg har en ven hvis han bare lever,
   for syv aar siden jeg fik ham kjaer.
   Han reiste fra mig, men jeg vil vente,
   for hvis han lever, han trofast er." (A: 2; B,C: 4)

5. "Er det syv aar siden han drog ifra dig,
   saa sig hans minde et smukt farvel."
   "Jeg tror han lever, han har mit hjerte,
   og er han død: Gud annam' hans sjel!" (A; 3; B,C: 5)

6. Nu som han hørte hun var oprigtig,
   da kunde han ei fordølge sig:
   "Du faar belønning for huld og troskab,
   thi vennen lever saa lykkelig.

7. "Jeg er den ven som for syv aar siden,
   for syv aar siden drog over hav.
   Nu er jeg kommet for dig at favne,
   og indfri løftet jeg engang gav." (A: 5)

8. "Er du den ven som for syv aar siden,
   for syv aar siden drog over hav,
   saa vis mig haanden, saa vis mig fing'ren,
   saa vis mig ringen som jeg dig gav." (A: 6)

9. Saa tog han haanden udi sin lomme,
   der laa en ring av det røde guld:
   "Her ser du haanden, her ser du fing'ren!"
   Da hun saa ringen, hun faldt omkuld. (A,B,C: 6)

10. Saa tog han hende i sine arme,
    og kyssed hende en gang, to, tre,
    og sagde: "Jeg er den lykkeligste,
    thi jeg har fundet min kjaereste." (A,B,C: 7)

But the sailors were not the only source of folk tradition on Tristan da Cunha. Supplementing and partly reinforcing this international tradition of the seven seas, important contributions appear to have been made by American whalers. Some of the New Englanders hunting for whale in the waters around Tristan were regular visitors to the island, returning year after year, and quite a few of them apparently stayed on shore long enough at least to go courting, as witnessed by the fact that several of William Glass' eight daughters and a few other Tristan girls left the island as brides of New England whalers. Some of these Americans even stayed on Tristan for several years, and three or four of them settled for life. Besides, many a young man of Tristan would get a job in a whaling sloop, some of them returning to Tristan to resettle after spending perhaps a number of years with relatives in New London or New Bedford.

Apparently, these whalers made an impact upon the community of Tristan da Cunha in various ways. The clergymen occasionally sent out by the Society for the Propagation of the Gospel seem to have experienced some frustration from them. The Rev. William F. Taylor, who stayed on Tristan from 1851 to 1857 as the first resident minister of the island, relates after having told of the arrival of the five women from St. Helena in 1827:

> Just after this, too, the island began to be much frequented by whale ships. This led to still further evil. Drunkenness, and other vices, began to prevail more among them, and consequently the highest duties of life could not fail to be so much the more neglected. The children that sprang from their union were badly cared for, and grew up mostly very ignorant. [19]

And the Rev. E. H. Dodgson, resident from 1880 to 1884, is reported by Peter Green to have said "that we [sinners at Tristan] are going to the devil — that is our young men that ship in them, i.e., in whale ships." [20] Peter Green himself seems to have had his troubles from the whalers, although for a different reason. In the letter just quoted, in which he protests sharply against Dodgson's suggestion that the island be evacuated and abandoned, he continues with some sarcasm:

> If Mr. Dodgson can get some of our people away from Tristan. I hope he will include the three whaling boys. One is an American, the other two are natives of Tristan, but they have spent the best part of their lives in whale ships. They have brought a very small stock of knowledge back to Tristan, and that is of a very vulgar kind. [21]

What kind of "small stock of knowledge . . . of a very vulgar kind" the whalers brought to Tristan, we can only guess. However, a considerable influence upon the song tradition of the island is apparent. In the first place, besides one whaling song, "Come all ye bold seamen," there were several songs of relatively recent American origin which unquestionably came to Tristan by direct import, such as the blackface minstrels "Old Dan Tucker" and "Girls from the South," which are known to have been picked up by an Islander, Tom Glass, during his whaling cruises. Furthermore, there is at least a possibility that some of the older songs with roots in the classical ballad tradition of England and Scotland may have been imported to Tristan by way of America, although it is practically impossible to determine with certainty the immediate source of any of these songs.

We may choose as an example the famous "Barbara Allen." The text of the Tristan version (p. 88) appears in part almost as an abbreviated variety of a traditional version from Virginia and would indicate a direct import from America. The Tristan version has only five stanzas, three of which appear as if they were lifted almost directly from the Virginia version. In Virginia they sang:

3. "Look up, look up at my bed-head,
    You'll see a napkin hanging;
    In that you'll find a gold watch and chain,
    And that's for Barbara Ellen.

4. "Look down, look down at my bed-foot,
    You'll see a trunk a-standing;
    It's full of gold and jewelry,
    And that's for Barbara Ellen."

. . . .

9. She went down into yonder vale;
    She could hear the dead-bell's knelling,
    And every toll it seemed to say,
    "Hard-hearted Barbara Ellen!" [22]

. . . .

And on Tristan da Cunha:

1. "Look down, look down by my bed-side,
    And there you'll find a basin
    With my gold watch and silver chain;
    Give that to Barv'ry Allen.

2. "Look down, look down by my bed-side,
    And there you'll find a towel
    With my gold watch and silver chain;
    Give that to Barv'ry Allen."

3. As I was walking in the church yard,
    I heard those bells a-tolling,
    And as they tolled, they seemed to say:
    "Cruel-hearted Barv'ry Allen!"

. . . .

Both versions emphasize the gifts from the dying hero to the undeserving girl. This motif is categorically rejected by Child as secondary — which indeed it may be — and, therefore, "unauthentic."[23] The impression is sometimes given that it is particularly characteristic of American versions of the song.[24] However, the motif is found in none of the sixteen variants of "Barbara Allen" presented in Sharp's collection of English folk songs from the southern Appalachian Mountains.[25] And of the nearly two hundred renditions presented by Bronson, almost two thirds of which are American, the gift motif is found in only seven cases, five of which were recorded in England, one in Scotland, and one in America (Maine).[26] And the English versions of the gift motif do not differ much in form from the Tristan and Virginia versions, as shown by the following example from Oxfordshire (Bronson's No. 133):

> 5. Now you look over my bedside,
>   You'll see my waistcoat hanging
>   With my gold watch and silver chain.
>   Give these to Barbara Allen.

Also the bell motif, which is almost universal with this song, occurs with little variation of form in British as well as American versions and gives us no clue to the immediate source of the Tristan rendition.

It may be worth noting that another American version, from Cambridge (Massachusetts) — originally, it seems, from Salem, the whaling center — contains a stanza which is almost word for word identical with the last stanza of the Tristan variety. The Salem version was recorded by Linscott.

Salem:

> 3. "Dying. Oh, no! That ne'er can be—
>   One kiss from you would cure me."
>   "One kiss from me you ne'er shall get
>   If your very heart was breaking!" [27]

Tristan:

> 5. "Dying, oh no, that ne'er can be!
>   A kiss from you will cure me."
>   "A kiss from me you ne'er shall get—
>   Keep your poor heart from breaking!"

But, again, this is a motif which is repeated in almost identical wording in Scottish and English as well as in many American versions.

A comparison of tunes does not bring us much further in trying to determine the relative importance of the two main sources of the song tradition on Tristan da Cunha. Unfortunately, Tolman's rendition of "Barbara Allen" from Virginia does not include the tune. However, the Salem version presented by Linscott does appear with a tune which, in certain respects, is strikingly related to the tune of the Tristan version:

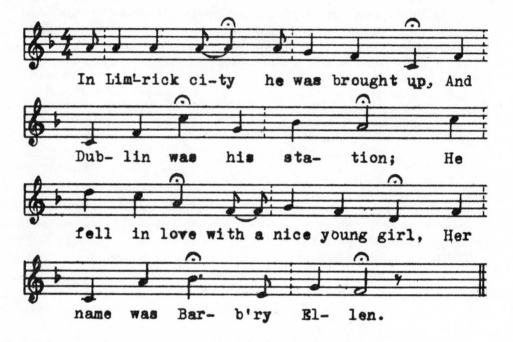

In Lim-rick ci-ty   he was brought up, And

Dub- lin was   his   sta-   tion;   He

fell in love with a nice young girl, Her

name was Bar- b'ry El- len.

The tune has a characteristic rhythm, which evidently was not easily submitted to the conventional common time meter, with a held note at every other stress, and with a semisyncopic effect toward the end of each cadence. This is the rhythmic pattern that we also find in the Tristan version: [28]

An identical rhythmic pattern is found in most of Sharp's sixteen variants of "Barbara Allen" from the southern Appalachian Mountains. Again, however, it is not a characteristic of American versions as distinct from the British. A similar pattern is actually predominant in a very large group of variants, with representatives found both in England and America (but relatively few in Scotland). A number of variants within this group are also melodically quite consistent. This is Bronson's "Group A," which he describes as follows:

> The first class [of variants] is quite consistently major, heptatonic, and fairly equally divided between authentic and plagal examples. It is *mainly English* [emphasis added], and many variants lean to 5/4 time, especially Sharp's tunes from Somerset. Its first-phrase final is likely to fall on the tonic. The authentic tunes move in the first phrase from tonic to dominant and back, rising in the second phrase to the octave but falling back for the middle cadence from VII to V, with feminine ending. The melodic curve of the third phrase imitates that of the second, and that of the fourth follows the first; but there is seldom an exact repetition, the pattern remaining ABCD. . . . [29]

The tune of the Tristan version fits this description exactly, with the only exception that it begins on the dominant.[30] This shows how close the Tristan tradition has remained to its roots, and since this melodic pattern is so very predominantly English, it may be taken as an argument for regarding "Barbara Allen" as a part of the British heritage that came to Tristan with the original settlers and the sailing ships. But it does not allow any conclusions concerning the rest of the songs of the ballad tradition.

It is of course impossible to determine how many of the songs current on Tristan da Cunha in 1938, or exactly which of them, were brought by American whalers and how many stem from the international tradition of the sailing ships. The two main sources of the song tradition of Tristan cannot be clearly separated for the simple reason that both of them have strong common roots in the British song tradition. The amazing tenacity of cultural tradition in general, as well as of the English heritage in particular, is brought to our attention when we consider how close the British colonial cultures, including the American, have stayed to the traditions of the mother country even in this respect. As far as it is possible at all to separate the two sources, it is perhaps fair to say that the songs of relatively recent origin — such as, notably, the songs of the minstrel shows of the middle and late nineteenth century — most likely came through the whaling traffic, while the typical sailor songs were the main contributions of the international but predominantly British tradition of the sailing ships. In the area of overlap between the two sources, particularly in the remnants of the old ballad tradition, they may mutually have reinforced each other.

*5. The Transmission Process
and the Authority of Tradition*

Traditional folk songs are, of course, always exposed to the hazards of oral transmission. Like other culture elements, therefore, living folk songs and other folk traditions are in a constant process of change. One important factor in this process of cultural innovation is undoubtedly some degree of inaccuracy in transmission by memory. No new generation remembers accurately the whole of its cultural heritage, and the more complex a culture is, the more likely is it to change simply through ordinary slips of memory.

The more remarkable is the great tenacity of *form* that is sometimes found in folk traditions, particularly in traditional songs. Even though a song may be subject to modifications and variations as it is transmitted through the generations and spread from one community to another, and even from one country to another, particular verbal phrases, or a certain rhythm or melodic pattern, may be retained with surprising consistency. In some cases, it appears that such a musical or verbal phrase may be inseparably associated with a particular song, almost like an indelible genetic trait. We have already seen how a great number of the recorded versions of "Barbara Allen" have retained a particular characteristic rhythmic pattern which clung to this song as it wandered practically from one end of the world to the other. Similarly, the whole mood and meaning of a song may be summed up, as it were, in a particular verbal phrase that thus becomes the very core around which the song may be variously built. "Barbara Allen," again, seems to have such a core phrase in the line where the hardhearted girl expresses her indifference to her lover's death by saying:

"Young man, I think you're dying."

Certainly, it is understandable that this very expressive line has been faithfully retained in most versions of the song both in Britain and in America, although otherwise the versions may vary greatly. As often as not, however, such "earmark phrases" are without any apparent cognitive significance or meaning. It is hard to explain, for instance, why "The Lexington Murder" always seems to take place "about eight o'clock at night," yet an indication of this particular time seems to be an earmark of this ballad and is retained consistently in a great many of its numerous versions, including the two recorded on Tristan da Cunha. The story of Sir Walter Raleigh's ship, recorded in the famous ballad "The Sweet Trinity" or "The Golden Vanity," was originally located on the coast of the Netherlands, and a reference to the "Lowlands low," reiterated in refrain-like fashion at the end of each stanza, has become the earmark of this ballad, although in most versions the name has lost all geographical significance. Even more striking is perhaps the fact that both in British and American versions of "The Lexington Murder," the name of the location fairly consistently contains the letter 'x' in the first syllable (Lexington, Oxford, Wexford, Woxford, Knoxville, etc.), or the girl is described, quite unintelligibly (as in one of the versions from Tristan, p. 71), as a "waxford" girl.

It is fairly obvious that such characteristics have been preserved by strictly *phonetic memory*, and it is quite likely that this type of memory plays a considerable part in the transmission of folk songs in general. The operation of phonetic memory was demonstrated several times during my collection of songs on Tristan da Cunha. More than once did I pose a question to my informants which they must have found rather naive or at least a bit strange, asking for the "meaning" of this or that unintelligible phrase in a song, and inevitably the answer was: "I don't know, Sir, it says so in the song." It is not that the cognitive meaning of a traditional song is insignificant. Most of these songs tell a recognizable story or contain intelligible lyrical descriptions of moods and sentiments. But apart from this, or perhaps even above this, it appears that every line or stanza of a song has a *musical* meaning, comprehended but not necessarily consciously intended or even recognized, in which melody, rhythm, and verbal modulation are more or less fused into a unit. "The textual line of the ballad, in singing," as Bronson puts it, "is seized by the ear as a *musical phrase.*" [31]

A purely phonetic transmission may often lead to distortions of the cognitive meaning, as demonstrated by many of the songs from Tristan da Cunha. Subject to such distortions are particularly those phrases in migratory songs which contain references to objects or situations unfamiliar to the local setting, or words that are strange to the local vocabulary and therefore meaningless. In such cases, the phonetic memory of form is not being supported by a cognitive memory of meaning. However, it is evidence of the importance of phonetic memory in the transmission of folk songs when such "empty" or meaningless forms are often faithfully retained with only slight phonetic distortions.

Two instances of this may be found in the Tristan version of "The Golden Vanity" (p. 75), where a presumably original "cashmere" has become "cashpere," while the "Tuckalivery" probably is a distorted derivation from the "Turkish galley" or something of that order. Another example, which clearly shows the subordination of cognitive meaning to what is conceived as the traditional phonetic form, may be seen in the Tristan version of "The Dying Californian" (p. 96), where the line, "Tell my mother — God assist her" [32] has become "Tell my mother — God resist her"!

From this point of view it is interesting to compare the Tristan version of the American blackface minstrel, "Josiphus Orange Blossom" (p. 109), with any printed text.[33] Henry Green used to perform this song, which was reported to have been introduced by a sailor on board the *Mabel Clark,* the American sailing ship which, as we recall, was wrecked at the island in 1878. Henry Green was then about fifteen years old, but it is not known whether he learned the song directly from the American sailor or from another Islander. In any case, the song has been preserved remarkably well in oral tradition for sixty years. And although such words and expressions as "play the possum," "contraband," "patronize," and "appall" obviously did not have a place in the vocabulary of Henry Green or the other Tristan Islanders, the nonsensical phonetic similitudes of these words are easily recognizable: "play the parson," "country band," "patridize," and "repall."

Another interesting example may be seen in the nonsensical lines of the last stanza of the Tristan version of "Sweet Pretty Polly Perkins from Paddington Green" (p. 100):

> For of ever'n he condunder
> out of two penny worth.

This, obviously, is what may happen to a "bow-legg'd conductor of a twopenny bus" in a community where a twopenny bus rings no bell, and where people probably would wonder what sort of thing a "conductor" is.

By this kind of phonetic memorizing, a song may occasionally be transmitted in a language that is completely incomprehensible to the singer as well as to his audience. An example of this from Tristan da Cunha is the following fragment of an "Italian" song, presented by Andrew Swain, the fiddler, whose diction, by the way, was not much better than that of his brother Ben, and whose pitch was considerably worse than that of his fiddle:

No Italian, to be sure, would recognize this as his native tongue. This is what happens when phonetic memory gets no support at all from the cognitive memory of meaning.

If the distortion is not too far gone, a creative soul may come into the line of transmission at this point and restore a cognitive meaning (although probably not the original one). However, phonetic memory and the power of formal tradition may be at work even here. How closely such restorations may stick to a traditional (but vaguely remembered) phonetic pattern is shown by a couple of examples from Tristan da Cunha. In "Maria Martini" (the Tristan variety of "The Lexington Murder"), the "waxford" girl of one version has been turned into a "waxen" girl in the other (p. 73). Particularly interesting are two versions of the first line of stanza 5 in "The Girl I Left Behind" (p.85). From the highly literate Frances Repetto (who nevertheless gave me the "waxford" version of "Maria Martini"), I obtained this line:

I advanced a little farther, finding the news was true,

while her illiterate brother, Henry Green, turned out the following version, which may be seen as the result of a combination of a half-forgotten phonetic form and the quest for some kind of cognitive meaning:

I went see her little father, find if the thing be true. [34]

It is generally recognized that folk songs, more than nonmusical folk traditions, may transmit memories of historical events with amazing accuracy. No doubt, it is the combination of phonetic and cognitive memory that brings this result. An extremely well preserved song, although set in a situation and describing events that definitely went beyond the limited experience of the Tristan Islanders, is "Little Powder-Monkey Jim" (p. 47). The song, obviously, is a British Navy song, and it is a good example of how faithfully orally transmitted folk songs may retain the record of an historical episode, even if removed to a milieu in which the event no longer has historical significance. The principal character of the song is a lowly "powder-monkey," a handyman in the powder magazine of a man-of-war, who was killed in action, and the main theme is clearly a character description rather than an epic narrative. A specific time and place would seem to have little bearing on the main theme of the song. Yet the situation is described with such accuracy that we can identify the particular naval battle in which the scene is set:

1. A yarn I've got to spin – it's how I heard my old Dad tell –
   Of a gallant little hero who on board the *Victory* fell.
   . . . .
2. In ninety-eight we chased the foe right into Bony Bay,
   We fought away like Niggers all the night till break of day.
   Our foeman's flagship *Orient* was blown away sky-high,
   The Admiral and all his crew, and serve them right, said I! [35]

The battle referred to is clearly the famous Battle of the Nile on August 1st and 2nd, 1798, in which Rear Admiral Nelson defeated the French fleet under Vice Admiral Brueys in Aboukir Bay, just outside Alexandria. In May of that year, Nelson received orders "to proceed in quest of the armament preparing by the enemy at Toulon and Genoa" and, if necessary, to follow the enemy "to any part of the Mediterranean or even into the Black Sea." Arriving off Toulon on May 31st, he found that the French fleet had already departed for an unknown destination. Guided by scant intelligence and by guesses based on observations of wind directions, Nelson went in pursuit and finally, after a two months' search, came upon the French fleet at anchor in Aboukir Bay, which was then, like Alexandria, held by the French and fortified. Says the song:

> In ninety-eight we chased the foe right into Bony Bay. [36]

Nelson stood in and, apparently to the surprise of the French Vice Admiral, attacked at sunset. The ensuing battle has been described as one of the fiercest battles in which the British Navy had ever been engaged. Involved were fifteen British and seventeen French ships, most of them large, mounting seventy-four or more guns each. Nelson anchored his ships broadside to the French line, and the two fleets engaged each other in an unceasing fire all through the night until well after daybreak, when the last four ships of the French line managed to escape:

> We fought away like Niggers all the night till break of day.

The outstanding event of the battle has been described by William Laird Clowes, historian of the British Navy, in his words:

> . . . But before the *Franklin* [a French 80-gunner] was silenced there happened an event of so awful a character as for a time to paralyze, as it were, both fleets.
> The French flagship *Orient* was first sought out by the *Bellerophon*, which anchored close alongside of the great three-decker, but which soon found the position untenable. By 7:50 P.M. the British 74 had lost her mizen mast; a little later her main mast went over the starboard bow, and she caught fire in several places, and at 8:20 P.M., being absolutely disabled, she set her sprit-sail, cut her stern cable, and got clear. . . . The attack upon the *Orient* was almost instantly taken up by the *Swiftsure* and the *Alexander;* and at 9 P.M. the former vessel perceived the French flagship to be on fire. The *Swiftsure* concentrated as much of her broadside as possible upon the burning spot, and thus probably interfered with the attempts to extinguish the flames. . . . The flames increased and spread along the deck and leapt up the rigging. Foreseeing the inevitable catastrophe, all the vessels near the doomed three-decker either shifted their berths, or, closing their ports and hatchways, and removing all ammunition from their upper decks, held in readiness large bodies of men with filled buckets. At about 10 P.M. the *Orient* was blown into the air by the explosion of her magazine. The concussion alone was so violent as to seriously injure ships which lay even at some distance; and the hurtling fragments of spars and wreckage presently fell a burning shower all around. Some fell in the *Swiftsure,* some in the *Alexander,* but most in the *Franklin.* The latter two vessels were set on fire; yet in both cases the flames were quickly extinguished. [37]

Thus runs the dramatic account of the historian. Curtly, the song reports:

> Our foeman's flagship *Orient* was blown away sky-high. The Admiral and all his crew, and serve them right, said I!

With amazing accuracy has this song, recorded on Tristan da Cunha in 1938, retained the following details of an event that took place at a distant location one hundred and forty years earlier: the year of the battle; the preceding chase, the location of the battle in a harbor controlled by Bonaparte; the time of day and duration of the battle, the fact that it was fought during the night; the name of the enemy's flagship and its fate. Most striking is perhaps the recollection of the name of the French flagship, the *Orient,* for the ship was known under that name only for a few months before she was destroyed. "She had previously been known as the *Sans Culotte,* and had been renamed in honour of the object of the expedition." [38]

The song is historically incorrect on one point. The *Victory,* although in existence at the time, did not take part in the Battle of the Nile. In this famous battle, Nelson had his flag in the *Vanguard.* However, the mention of the *Victory* in this song may be of more than passing interest. In the first place, it is obviously an instance of the well-known tendency for tales to converge upon mythically significant locations, in this case the famed *Victory,* Nelson's flagship in the Battle of Trafalgar seven years later. Secondly, since this song was frequently performed by Fred Swain and was considered "his" song, we are reminded of the fact that Fred's great-grandfather, Thomas Swain, was believed to have served in the *Victory* under Nelson and was even identified as the sailor who caught the mortally wounded Admiral in his arms as he fell on the deck of that famous ship. On that account, the song may have had a particular significance to the Tristan Islanders, and it was with some pride that Fred Swain regarded it as "his" song.

Generally, the songs of Tristan da Cunha seemed to have been transmitted rather faithfully in the form in which they were received, or at least in the form in which they were remembered, with hardly an attempt being made to recreate a cognitive meaning lost in the process. Tradition is the ultimate authority – "it says so in the song!" This deference to tradition, as we have seen, is a general trait with the Tristan Islanders, at least as we saw them in 1938, and is undoubtedly related to their isolation. [39] Of course, the trait is not peculiar to Tristan; indeed, a combination of traditionalism and relative isolation is a determining characteristic of all folk societies. [40] But traditionalism may have been more pronounced in Tristan da Cunha than in most communities of the Occidental culture area simply because here we have an extreme case of isolation.

Such deference to tradition may indeed ensure the preservation of culture forms which may have been removed from the context of their original meaning – and this is not limited to folk cultures (in Redfield's sense) but may also apply to certain sacrosanct culture forms of "higher" and more complex civilizations, as witnessed by the role of the Christmas tree in modern Western society, completely divorced, not only from its original pagan significance as a symbol of vitality, but also from its secondary Christian interpretation. By the same token, the Tristan Islanders have preserved fairly well, despite distortions that do occur, a number of songs whose contents go far beyond the limited range of their own physical and social environment, and whose words may be strange to the local vocabulary. If one asked for the meaning of the texts they sang, they did not always know. Yet the prototype of a good singer was one who performed and transmitted his songs in the traditional form, even though the text might be partly unintelligible to him and his audience. The authority of tradition, here as elsewhere, appears to be more concerned with the form than with the contents of culture.

Against this background, it can hardly be a surprise to find a complete absence of original songs endemic to Tristan da Cunha. This, I believe, is not a matter of intelligence and artistic sensitivity.[41] Artistic creativity, although usually an individual performance, is, like any form of cultural creation and innovation, a complex social process. Among the most important factors in this process is a community situation open to new impulses from cultural diffusion, and with a positive attitude toward the new and original. Even under more favorable conditions than those of Tristan da Cunha, one can surely not expect a great amount of cultural originality in most communities of a comparable size. If indeed a problem is to be seen in the absence of endemic songs on Tristan (or of any form of original art expression), it is clearly related to the general conservative and traditional character of the community, which in turn is a result of its high degree of isolation.

6. Ballads and Other Songs

An important factor of change in the transmission of cultural traditions is the influence of new styles and tastes, which may come about through a complex process of cultural diffusion, and which is checked and kept in balance only by the authority of tradition itself. Under conditions of extensive intercultural contacts, this influence is generally strong and may promote conscious innovations, often at the very limit of what tradition will consider proper – or slightly beyond it as in the case of fad and fashion. The result, of course, is a relatively rapid rate of change.

In a genuine folk society, however, where the flow of cultural transfusion is relatively slow and limited, and where the power of tradition is generally strong, the influence of new styles and tastes may nevertheless work in a number of more subtle ways to bring about a more or less unconscious adaptation of traditional ideas, customs, and forms of expression. An important factor here is the *selective* nature of human memory. Traditional ideas and forms of expression which are *meaningful*, both in a cognitive and an aesthetic way, are more readily remembered, while less meaningful traditions may be recalled only in a slightly modified form or sink into oblivion, the gaps being filled if necessary, by imagined "recollections" which are, in fact, the joint products of half-forgotten tradition and demands for cognitive and aesthetic meaning.

In folk singing, as outmoded or meaningless and phonetically (but imperfectly) remembered forms are restored to new life, and as forgotten (or discarded) bits and phrases are replaced, new styles and tastes, perhaps vaguely conceived, may exert their influence. As a result, the product may slowly change into something very different but aesthetically more meaningful to the new generation. This is what Lomax is referring to when he says:

> In this way an extraneous element may enter a stanza and will alter it completely, as successive singers try to rationalize the irrational element. This is one of the processes of *creative forgetting* by which folk singers slowly modernize and protect the valued old songs. [42]

It has often been stated that the epical ballad of the seventeenth and eighteenth centuries, with its straight narrative style, sometimes harshly realistic, does not usually dwell upon the moods and feelings of its characters but lets the story speak for itself, with the dramatic high points often rendered in the form of a pert dialogue. There may be romance and passion, but often frustrated in the face of the realities of moral codes and social convention. And even if the rose and the briar may intertwine in the end, the message of the ballad is mostly moral and impersonal rather than romantic and sentimental. Moreover, the music seemed to confirm and emphasize this epical style. The old ballad tunes — based perhaps originally on pentatonic scales with more or less vague gap-fillers or "grace notes," particularly for the larger intervals [43] — have a certain flexibility of melody and rhythm which sometimes almost gives the ballad when performed, the character of a *recitativo*, or even a *parlando*, and allows a complete fusion of cognitive and musical meaning, with the musical phrase clearly subordinate to the verbal phrase which it supports. Cecil Sharp was aware of this intimate relationship between words and music in the typical ballad and stated that "the most perfect type of ballad . . . is that in which the tune, whilst serving its purpose as an ideal vehicle for the words, is of comparatively little value when divorced from its text." [44]

The romantic movement, which was not an exclusive fad of intellectuals and artists but carried itself with great force to the very grass roots of Western culture, shifted the emphasis to sentimental rather than cognitive, to subjective rather than objective values, and eventually brought about a change in the style of the popular song no less than of other art forms. The epical drama *en miniature*, which the typical ballad had presented, was replaced by the affective mood of the romance, in which the lyrical description of character, of sentiments and feelings, became the main thing, while an epical element, if present at all, might play an entirely subordinate role. And as the music was emancipated, as it were from the epical drama even at the folk level of culture, there emerged the sentimental lyrical air of the typical nineteenth century popular song with its melodic *cantabile*, in which the function of the verbal phrase might be reduced to giving modulation and lyrical support to the musical phrase. Such an air might indeed live a life of its own, attaching itself now to one, then to another text; or it might become completely independent of any text, as happened often enough when song tunes were adapted to the accordion, which more and more replaced the fiddle as the dominant instrument of musical folk tradition.

What happened to the old ballads in this changing climate of folk tradition is plain to see. Since they no more met the aesthetic demands of the time, most of them were either forgotten, ejected from the memory of folk tradition; or they were transformed, more or less successfully adapted to the romantic style and taste of a later period.[45] Only in the back eddies of the evolutionary stream of culture did the old ballads stay on in the old style as living folk tradition — until they were rediscovered by sages and scholars, analyzed and dissected, and then put in permanent storage in voluminous collections along with variants and learned commentary.

That this development meant a deterioration of the old ballad style can hardly be doubted — such is the nature of cultural change. This observation does not imply, however, that what developed in the place of the old ballad was necessarily inferior in aesthetic quality. And it certainly did not mean the end of folk singing. A change in values, such as always occurs in cultural evolution, calls for new forms of expression, and a judgment about the superior quality of one form over another depends on the value system used as a measure. It is quite understandable that to the scholarly folklorists of Europe and America, who in general share the value system of the Western academic world with its emphasis on the classical virtues of rationality and constraint, romanticism in its purest and most exuberant form, and particularly folk romanticism, may appear as a cheap and vulgar overindulgence in primitive sentimentaltiy. However, when the popular songs of the nineteenth century are seen within the framework of their own inherent value system, it is quite conceivable that some real gems of folk art may still be found, although they may not appeal to the more "sophisticated" taste of present-day scholars.[46]

Taking into consideration the fact that the Tristan community does not have a very long history of undisturbed tradition relatively removed from the mainstreams of cultural diffusion and change but was actually shaped during the nineteenth century as a living part of the exciting life of the high seas, it should not be surprising to find that the songs of this community, whether old or new, mostly appear in a verbal and musical form which clearly points to the romantic taste and style of the nineteenth century. On the other hand, survivors from an earlier period, more or less well preserved, are found even here and, generally, the songs current on Tristan da Cunha may be seen to represent various stages in the development from the epical ballad to the lyrical romance.

Probably the best example of a fairly well preserved ballad in the old style is "Maria Martini," the Tristan version of "The Lexington Murder" (p. 71). The song is closely related to a number of "murdered lady ballads,"[47] notably to "The

Lexington Miller," from the Harvard collection of broadsides.[48] Already there is some deviation from the classical ballad style. A subjective element, as it were, is introduced by rendering the story in the first person. Lost is also some of the dramatic tension of the old ballad by leaving out the motivation for the murder, which originally may have been to evade the obligation of marrying a girl made pregnant.[49] And there is no supernatural avenger, such as is often found in the older ballads. Instead, there is a rather prosaic reference to the arrest and conviction of the murderer. On the whole, however, the story is straightforward and kept in a simple narrative style, with some dramatic detail that is almost gruesome to our taste because it is told without compassion. And the message is stern and callous:

> Come all ye young and silly young men,
> Take warning unto this,
> And never do no murder
> For to be hung like me.

To a modern taste, the song has a sombre character, which is greatly emphasized by its pentatonic Dorian mode.[50]

There were even a few other songs on Tristan da Cunha that were preserved in the old ballad modes. However, they were mostly obtained from the older people, and they were not among the most frequently performed songs. Illustrations may be seen in two untitled songs, both obtained from Henry Green. One, mentioned above, was a version of a song which, according to Lomax, "has been cherished by the restless, footloose Anglo-American tribe for almost three centuries,"[51] known in many parts of the United States as "The Girl I Left Behind" (p. 85). On Tristan, this song was rendered in what appears to be a plagal tune in a peculiar hexatonic mode. The other example was a somewhat garbled version in a Mixolydian mode of the old favorite, "Oh No, John," which, however, had lost its original point because the famous refrain had dropped out (p. 90). Some of these old songs had lost part or all of their stories in the process of transmission, apparently through lack of regular use, leaving in some cases a rather incoherent text.

Many of the classical ballads. however, survived the transition in style and taste, and retained their popularity in the English speaking world by going through a more or less extensive adaptation, particularly to the melodic demands of the romantic period. Among the songs current on Tristan, "The Turkish Lady" (p. 77) offers a good example. Like most of the numerous nineteenth century versions of this song, it is quite far removed from the famous classical ballad of "Young Beichan." But it still relates a meaningful story which must have had a particular appeal to the romantic taste, showing — as it does — how true love is *not* frustrated but finds its way successfully through the obstacles of social convention and religious intolerance. And the tune has the melodic quality characteristic of the nineteenth century romance, although it does not quite reach the flowing sweetness of the typical sailor song.

It is reasonable to assume that the more popular a song is, the more will it be subject to adaptations according to changes in style and taste. What may happen to a very popular old ballad in this respect may be illustrated again by the Tristan version of "Barbara Allen" (p. 88). On account of its great popularity, its wide distribution, and its frequent use in various parts of the English-speaking world, this song may be assumed to have gone through an exceptionally large number of oral transmissions before it reached Tristan da Cunha. In fact, the Tristan version is quite corrupt, almost rudimentary. Of its five stanzas two are only slightly incremental repetitions of the preceding stanzas. The epical element of the old Scottish ballad has practically disappeared. It is as if the singer would merely suggest a story too well known to be repeated, the more to dwell upon the moods of his characters, the touching faithfulness of the dying lover, and the cold indifference of the cruel-hearted girl, the whole presented in a somewhat incoherent dialogue form. Also, the song was rendered in a tune which, in spite of its unusual rhythm, carries many of the characteristics of the romantic melodic air and which stands in sharp contrast to the modal sternness typical of the older Scottish versions.

As another example of an extensive adaptation of style, it may be of interest in this connection to note that a more recent version of "Oh No, John," the famous refrain included, was very popular on Tristan and well known by all, especially the last (and probably secondary) stanza, from which the song was mostly referred to simply as "Lady Dear" (p. 93). This version was so different from the old incomplete version sung by Henry Green (p. 90) that it was not even recognized as the same song.

Naturally, in the adaptation of a song from one style to another, something may get lost in the process. It is not surprising, therefore, to find that those songs which are the original products of the romantic period are generally better preserved on Tristan as complete compositions. This is not only because they are younger but particularly because, in a community where they are still a part of living tradition, their original style is still the preferred style.

A good example of a complete and well-preserved song in what appears to be a transitional style between ballad and romance is "Little Powder-Monkey Jim" (p. 47). As we have seen, the song actually refers to an historical event and relates a tale associated with it. But, although the situation is described with some specificity, the accent of the tale is not on the specific actions or events. Clearly, the epical element of the song, such as it is, is only of secondary importance and quite subordinate to the more universal description of the cheerful character and the gallant courage of the little hero, presented with a definite touch of sympathetic sentiment.

Entirely a product of the romantic taste of the nineteenth century, and typical of the sentimental sailor songs that were so popular on Tristan da Cunha as well as in the whole pelagic culture of the seven seas, is another song of Fred Swain's, sung to me by his daughter Alice (p. 58). The song was given no title; but a rudimentary version of it has been recorded in Newfoundland under the title "The Sailor Boy," and this is the title that we shall give it here. An epical element may be seen even in this song in that it relates the story of a sailor and his girl saying good-bye on "one dark and stormy winter's night" and what happened when "the ship returned without her sailor boy." But the situation as well as the characters are general rather than specific. What the song relates is not what happened once upon a time to a specific sailor and his sweetheart, but rather what happens over and over again and may in fact happen to every young sailor on the sea and to every sweetheart left behind. There is tenderness and deep sentiment in the parting words, which are effectively repeated in the form of a full-length refrain, like an echoed recollection in the girl's heart as she hears about her lover's death at sea. And the tune is sweet and melodic, held in the moderate 6/8 meter of the two-step waltz which is known in many lands as the typical "sailor waltz." William Doerflinger, who recorded and published the Newfoundland version of the song, describes it as "a dogwatch favorite in British vessels" and relates: "Captain James P. Barker once told me that when he first shipped out under sail, in the 1880s, there was a little French sailor in the crew who often sang 'The Sailor Boy' with tears running down his face." [52]

With this and similar songs – like "A Light in the Window" (p. 60) and "The Ship that Never Returned" (p. 62) as well as the gayer "Little Annie Rooney" (also a typical sailor waltz) – we are at the end of the line of transition that led from the epical ballad to the lyrical romance so dear to the sailor. Other lines of transition led to the development of the humorous and sentimental music-hall songs of England – like Harry Clifton's "Sweet Pretty Polly Perkins of Paddington Green" (p. 100) or "After the Ball" (p. 124) –and the very American blackface minstrel songs, which seem to have been the beginning of American show business and comedianship. And somehow, all of them found their way to Tristan da Cunha.

Obviously, the Tristan community played only a passive and receiving role in these developments. Here, as we have seen, the songs were generally transmitted rather faithfully as best they were recalled, even if the sounds were strange and the contents unfamiliar. Under these circumstances, distortions easily occur, as amply demonstrated by the songs of Tristan da Cunha.

On the other hand, given a cultural milieu in which to remain comprehensible and meaningful, old styles and forms of cultural expression are more accurately preserved under the conditions of relative isolation from the mainstreams of cultural transfusion, as every collector of folklore material is aware. In the case of Tristan da Cunha, the isolation is of comparatively recent date. One could hardly expect, therefore, to find eighteenth century ballads untainted by the popular style of a later period. However, as the isolation grew more pronounced toward the end of the nineteenth century to become nearly complete during the first four decades of the twentieth century, the island was left in a situation where it was out of reach of the newest developments in popular song style dispersed throughout the world by mechanical recording and electronic transmission, and where sea and sail continued to form an integral part of everyday life. It was this situation which made the Tristan community a residual of the pelagic traditions of the nineteenth century. Best preserved, therefore, are those songs which concur fully with the romantic style and taste of that century and of those traditions, especially if the songs are concerned with things familiar to the Islanders, such as the joys and tragedies of the high seas.

7. Ditties and Dance Tunes

As already mentioned, singing on Tristan da Cunha usually took the form of a *performance* and was generally associated with certain social situations. It required an attentive audience, large or small, and a solo performer who was himself, restricted by certain rules of propriety that required him, for instance, to stay within the repertoire of songs which were commonly recognized as "his" songs. Also, the performer was expected to present his songs in a consistent form, and most singers apparently were quite conscious of this expectation, taking it almost as an obligation, not so much to the audience as to himself as a singer and to tradition. In other words, the singer is consciously performing a role, and the song he presents is an intrinsic part of that role.[53] We have already seen how this may be an important factor in the preservation of a traditional song in a given phonetic form.

There was, however, another category of songs that seemed to have a less pretentious place in the cultural heritage of the community. These were the lesser songs and ditties − shorter, often fragmentary and sometimes non-sensical lines and tunes that were never performed in front of an audience, that did not "belong" to any one in particular but were floating around freely, quoted on pertinent occasions, and sung or lilted by children during their play and by women as they did their chores around the house.

Most of these ditties and fragments were obviously of more recent origin, including even a well known favorite of the First World War (No.16A, p. 127), and to all appearance they were a much less stable element in the tradition of the Tristan community than were the more formal songs. Some of them seemed to have come about through a corruption and reduction of complete songs, such as often may be the case with nursery rhymes, game songs, and ditties in folk tradition.[54] From this point of view, "After the Ball" (No. 13, p. 124), "All Under the Coconut Tree" (No. 14, p.125), and "Say, Boys" (No.15, p. 127), as presented below, may be regarded as songs in various stages of corruption, although it is not known whether the reduction took place before or after the songs reached Tristan da Cunha. In these songs, the cognitive meaning of the text has been more or less abandoned, and the songs had obviously lost all significance as songs to be performed before an audience. What has saved them from complete oblivion is probably the fact that the tunes had acquired a new significance to the Islanders. Most of the ditties current on

Tristan in 1938 had been converted into dancing tunes, adapted mostly to the accordion but also to the fiddle, thus completing the emancipation of music from text. And it was obvious that these tunes were much more important to the Islanders as dancing tunes than they were as songs; in fact, most of them were construed by the Islanders to be original dancing tunes to which some silly words had been attached.[55]

To be convertible into a dance tune, a song obviously had to fit into a certain rhythmical pattern. In this respect the Tristan tradition was as firmly established as in anything else, and even here the pattern seemed to be that of the late nineteenth century. The most popular dance was the two-step "waltz" which, as often as not, was danced to a common-time rhythm rather than to the usual triple time. But there were also a number of older dances such as, notably, the schottische or, as the Islanders called it, the "shottee," and the "step-dance."

Most of the older dances, as might be expected, were figure dances which originally may have involved a number of movements, usually alternating with a basic movement exhibiting the basic steps of the particular dance. A show performance of the step-dance, given for the benefit of the members of the Norwegian expedition by some of the older people, including Frances Repetto, Jane Lavarello, Old Sam Swain, Henry Green, and others, and with Andrew Swain playing the fiddle, showed a pattern of various movements in which the dancers exchanged partners and interchanged places, but always reverted for the first eight bars of the tune to the basic pattern of partners dancing opposite each other in two rows. Andrew Swain played the tune here presented as No.2 (p.118), with its characteristic extra beat on the last note, allowing the dancers — with a loud stamp and a shout — to take their places after each rearrangement.

The older Islanders named a number of different dances that they used to dance, each with its peculiar characteristics. However, in the course of time, the various dances had nearly all converged into a fairly stereotypical pattern involving usually no more than two alternating movements, the "stepping part" and the "swinging part," each indicated by a distinct melodical pattern of the corresponding part of the tune. Accordingly, the step-dance as performed by the younger crowd had been reduced to a relatively simple pattern of two movements, the basic "stepping part" and just one variety of the "swinging part" in which the partners would swing around with interlocked arms. And the Tristan concept of the "waltz" probably developed from a number of originally distinct coupled figure dances converging into a similar generalized pattern, which also embraced and changed the original triple-time waltz-in-the-round and molded it into the same stereotypical form, with a "stepping part" and a "swinging part." This may explain the fact that on Tristan we find "waltzes" in common as well as in triple time.[56] In this case, the "stepping part" simply consists of the usual two-steps or three-steps, as the case may be, alternatingly to the left and right without "swinging."

A few dances had retained many of their peculiar characteristics in spite of the generalizing tendency, perhaps because of the clearness with which the melodic figures indicate the steps. An example is "Tapioca's Big Toe"(No. 7, p. 121),with its three movements, each with its distinct rhythmical pattern closely indicating the steps, and with its characteristic shift from triple to common and back to triple time in the first movement.[57] Other examples are the "Heel-Toe Polka"(No. 8, p. 122)and the "waltz," No. 9 (p. 122), which is closely similar to "Tapioca's Big Toe" in the basic figure of steps.

In the dances just mentioned, each figure of steps is inseparably associated with a particular musical figure. A substitution of the tune, therefore, is out of question unless the new tune be so similar to the old one as to be almost identical. It is only in the generalized dances, particularly in the "waltz," that the opportunity for substitution exists without changing the basic character of the dance. But even here the demands for a particular rhythmic pattern are fairly strict.

The "ideal" dance tune on Tristan da Cunha thus consists of two parts with related and yet distinct rhythmic and melodic patterns, the first part serving always as the "stepping part" and the second as the "swinging part" of the dance. Preferably, the two parts should be equal in length, each comprising four, eight, or sixteen bars. At least, the number of stresses in each part should be even so as to allow the dancers to enter the next part "right," i.e., on the left foot for the man and on the right foot for his partner.

Few song tunes actually fit this pattern, and this may be the reason why some song tunes known on Tristan, which in many respects would seem eminently suited for dancing, never entered the dance hall. Particularly the demand for two different parts seems to have been important and may have been a factor in making "Little Annie Rooney" (p.98), with its musically distinct refrain, one of the most popular dance tunes(p.124),while "The Sailor Boy" (p.58), which has a swaying rhythm and which we have described as a typical "sailor waltz," apparently never was considered for dancing because its refrain simply repeats the air with a uniform rhythmic and melodic pattern throughout. Possibly for the same reason, Andrew Swain never had much success at the dance with "All Under the Coconut Tree" (No. 14, p. 125), although he occasionally played it on his fiddle.

However, once the requirement of two melodically and rhythmically distinct parts was met, the otherwise highly conventional patterns of the Tristan community apparently allowed the musician a certain amount of freedom in adapting a traditional tune to his instrument and to the rhythmical demands of the dance. Occasionally, he might even create a missing "swinging part," as may have been the case with Nos. 1B (p. 117), 3B (p. 119), and 18B (p. 130). And he might feel free to invert the order of the two parts, as in the case of No.16B (p. 128),where the first part of the corresponding song tune (No.16A, p. 127) has become the "swinging part" while the refrain has been used for the "stepping part." There were also frequent deviations from the demand for equal length of the two parts. Sometimes either part might be twice the length of the other (e.g., "Little Annie Rooney," No. 12, p.124), sometimes one of the parts might be two or even four beats short or long (Nos. 10, p.123; 17, p. 129; 20, p. 131), which would give a peculiar semi-syncopic effect.

A modest amount of ornamentation was also allowed, perhaps even expected as a mark of a good player. This was particularly Alfred Green's forte, and it may have been a contributing factor in making him the most highly praised accordion player in the community and the unquestioned music master of the communal dances. Examples of his treatment may be seen in his version of "Little Annie Rooney" (No. 12, p. 124) and in No. 22B (p. 133) as compared with No. 22A (p. 132).[58]

A similar license seemed to pertain to rhythmic adaptations. These were always moderate, but more or less so depending on the rhythmical characteristics of the original tune. However, if we may judge from the limited number of examples available, there was usually not much originality in these adaptations. As far as an adjustment of the rhythmical mold of a given song tune was undertaken at all, it seemed to have a tendency to fall into an already familiar pattern. Thus the ditty, No. 1A (p.117) with its compound quadruple meter, was of course reminiscent of the step-dance, No. 2 (p.118), with its "dotted" 2/4 meter occasionally broken by a triplet, and this was the pattern the ditty assumed when adapted to the accordion (No.1B, p. 117). No.4 (p. 120) may in part have been the model in adapting No. 3A (p. 118) into a schottische (No. 3B, p.119), and No.18A (p. 130) naturally fell into a rhythmical pattern identical to that of the "stepping part" of No. 19 (p. 131) and so became the "stepping part" of No. 18B (p. 130). Perhaps even more striking is the adaptation of No. 16A (p.127) into the rhythmical pattern of No.16B (p. 128), which in the "stepping part" is identical and in the "swinging part" quite similar to the corresponding rhythmical patterns of No. 17 (p.129).[59] And these rhythmical imitations are only in part, if at all, explainable by the rhythmical demands of the particular dance.

Thus we find, even in an area where some freedom appeared to prevail for individual creativity, a strong adherence to established norms, to the extent that the innovations themselves are reduced to something little more than a rearrangement of familiar patterns. Again, as in the case of the absence of endemic songs, it is meaningless to ponder whether this adherence to established forms is due to a lack of creative ability in the individuals comprising the community or whether it stems from the social pressure of tradition. The one follows from the other. The traditionalism of a folk society leaves few avenues open to individual creativity and inventiveness.

SONGS OF THE SEVEN SEAS

Little Powder-Monkey Jim

Text and tune: Fred Swain.
For comments, see pp. 34-37, 40.

A yarn I've got to spin, it's how I heard my old Dad tell of a

gal-lant lit-tle he-ro who on board the *Vic-try* fell. He was

brim-men full of cour-age, he was just the sort of lad to

make the sort of sai-lor that our Na-vy al-ways had. Now

Lit-tle Pow-der Mon-key Jim was the pet of all the crew, with his

flax-en hair so cur-ly and his pret-ty eyes so blue. The

boat swain al-ways said that's how, that what got o-ver him, the

cho-rus of a sai-lor's song was sung by Lit-tle Jim:

Soon we'll be in Lon-don Town, Sing, ma lad-die, oh! to

see the King in his gol-den crown. Sing, ma lad-die, oh!

Hea' ho, on we go! Sing, ma lad-die oh!

Who's a-fear'd to me to foe! Sing, ma lad-die, oh! oh!

1. A yarn I've got to spin, it's how I heard my old Dad tell,
    Of a gallant little hero who on board the *Vict'ry* fell.
    He was brimmen full of courage, he was just the sort of lad
    To make the sort of sailor that our Navy always had.
    Now Little Powder-Monkey Jim was the pet of all the crew,
    With his flaxen hair so curly and his pretty eyes so blue.
    The bo's'n always said that's how, that what got over him,
    The chorus of a sailor's song was sung by Little Jim:
        Soon we'll be in London Town,
          Sing, ma laddie, oh!
        To see the King in his golden crown,
          Sing, ma laddie, oh!
        Hea' ho, on we go,
          Sing, ma laddie, oh!
        Who's afear'd to me to foe!
          Sing, ma laddie, oh, oh!

2. In ninety-eight we chased the foe right into Bony Bay,
    And we fought away like Niggers all the night till break of day.
    Our foeman's flagship *Orient* was blown away sky-high,

The Admiral and all his crew, and serve them right, said I.
Now Little Jim was in the thick of all the fire and smoke,
And seemed to think that fighting hard was nothing but a joke.
For he handed up the powder from the magazine below,
And all the while was singing as if his pluck to show:
    Soon we'll be in London Town, *etc.*

3. Now Little Jim was book' for us, the fight was just on won,
   And the musket bullet picked him off before the song was sung.
   They carried him to a cockpit, and a-smiling he did lie;
   The sailor: "Well, there went a man." Somehow he pipe' his eye.
   "Ma lad," says Jim, "don't fret for me, but if the shore she see,
   Give a kiss to dear old Mother and say it come from me."
   For it never was a braver heart could serve our gracious King
   Than Little Powder-Monkey who so gayly used to sing:
     Soon we'll be in London Town, *etc.*

Henry Dear

Text: Frances Repetto (in writing).
Tune: Alice Swain (Glass).
    The first phrase of the tune is similar, and the second phrase identical, to that of "The Butcher Boy," also obtained from Alice Swain (p. 80).
    For the text, cf. "The Sailor Boy" (Leach, 1955, p. 736 f.; Laws, 1957, p. 146).
    6/3 should probably read:
            Saying, "Happy, happy, o, is the bride"

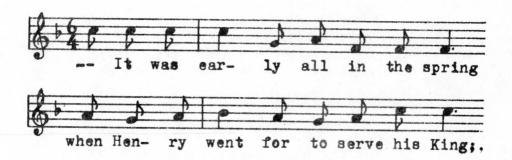

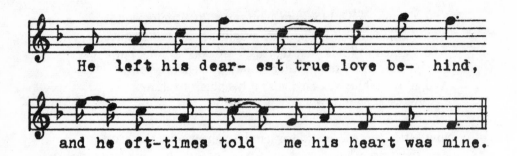

He left his dear- est true love be- hind,

and he oft-times told me his heart was mine.

1. It was early all in the spring,
   when Henry went for to serve his King;
   He left his dearest true love behind,
   · and he ofttimes told me his heart was mine.

2. Come all you sailors, stand in a row,
   my Henry he is the greatest I how,
   He's the greatest show, o, amongst them all,
   if I don't have him, I'll have none at all.

3. Come build for me a little boat,
   that I may on the wide ocean float
   And view the shipping as we pass by.
   Come and weep for me and my sailor boy.

4. I had not gone far across the sea,
   before some Queen's ship I chance to meet.
   "Say, Captain, Captain, come tell me true,
   Is my sweet sailor among your crew?"

5. "Oh no, fair lady, he is not here,
   oh yes, fair lady, he is drowned I fear;
   'Tis yonder green island as we pass by,
   it was there we lost your sweet sailor boy."

6. She wrung her hands and she tore her hair
   like some poor virgin in deep despair,
   Saying, "Happy, happy, o, is the girl
   that have her true love down by her side."

7. She sat right down and she wrote a song,
   she wrote it true and she wrote it long,
   And on every line she did drop a tear,
   and on every verse she cried Henry dear.

Her Sailor Boy

Text: A, Lily Green (written down by Agnes Rogers);
      B, Lily Glass (Rogers);
      C, Alice Swain (Glass).
Tune: Alice Swain (Glass).
Cf. "The Bailiff's Daughter of Islington" (Child, No. 105; Coffin, 1950, p. 101 f.; Leach, 1955, p. 313 f.), "The Love Token" (Leach, 1955, p. 315), "A Sweetheart in the Army" (Leach, 1955, p. 701 ff.), "The Single Sailor" (Mackenzie, 1963, p. 168ff.).
Norwegian version: "For syv aar siden" (see p. 23f)

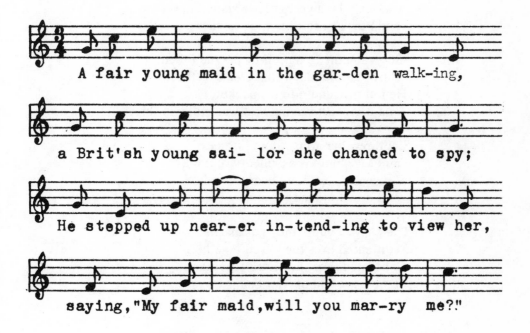

A fair young maid in the gar-den walk-ing,
a Brit'sh young sai- lor she chanced to spy;
He stepped up near-er in-tend-ing to view her,
saying,"My fair maid,will you mar-ry me?"

A

1. A fair young maid in the garden walking,
   a Brit'sh young sailor she chanced to spy.
   He stepped up nearer intending to view her,
   saying, "My fair maid, will you marry me?"

2. "I have a true love, kind Sir," she answered,
   "and sev'n long years he has been to sea,
   And sev'n years longer I'll wait upon him;
   if he's alive, he'll return to me."

3. "Sev'n long years make an alteration,
   he may be dead or he may be false;
   I'll marry you and make you my lady,
   with servants for to wait upon thee."

4. "A man of horror, a man of horror,
   a man of horror you seem to be!
   How can you impose upon a poor young woman,
   who is not fit for your servant to be?"

5. "I am your true love, my dear," he answered,
   "and sev'n long years I have been to sea,
   And sev'n long years I have waited upon thee,
   and now I've returned for to marry thee."

6. "Show me the token, show me the token,
   show me the token that I gave to thee."
   He put his hand into his pocket,
   and drew forth a ring that was broke in three.

7. She threw her arms round his neck,
   and gave him kisses, one, two, three,
   Saying, "You are my dear lost sailor,
   and now I'm ready to marry thee."

8. The happy couple they got married,
   contented lives they lived together,
   Contented lives they lived together;
   that is the end of 'Her Sailor Boy.'

                    B
1. A fair young maid in the garden walking,
   a Brit'sh young sailor I chanced to see;
   He was coming up intending to view me,
   saying, "My pretty miss, will you fancy me?"

2. A man of honour, a man of honour,
   a man of honour he seemed to me.
   "Oh, how can you apose on a poor young woman,
   who is not fit for your servant to be?"

3. "If I'm not fit for your servant to be,
   a great reward I have got for you;
   I'll marry you and make you my lady,
   and servants all for to wait on you."

4. "I have a true love, kind Sir," she answered,
   "he may be dead or he may be alive;
   But if he's alive, oh, I love him dearly,
   and if he's dead, he's an angel now.

5. "Oh, sev'n long years made a great alt'ration,
   he may be dead or he may be alive;
   But if he's alive, oh, I love him dearly,
   and if he's dead, he's an angel now."

6. He pulled his hand out of his pocket
   those pearly white fingers both long and thin;
   But when she saw, oh, the ring she gave him,
   she fall right down into his arms.

7. He picked her up and gave her kisses,
   and gave her kisses both one, two, three,
   Saying, "I'm your poor and lonely sailor,
   who have just returned from the raging sea."

8. Those lovely couple they got married,
   contented lives they did live together,
   Contented lives they did live together;
   and that's the end of 'My Sailor Boy.'

                        C
1. A fair young maid in the garden walking,
   a Brit'sh young sailor she chanced to see;
   He was coming up intending to view her,
   saying, "My pretty miss, can you marry me?"

2. A man of honour, a man of honour,
     a man of honour he seemed to be.
   "Oh, how can you apose on a poor young woman,
     who is not fit for your servant to be?"

3. "If I'm not fit for your servant to be,
     a great reward I have got for you;
   I'll marry you and make you my lady,
     and servants all for to wait on you."

4. "I have a true love, kind Sir," she answered,
     "he may be dead or he may be alive.
   But if he's alive, oh, I love him dearly,
     and if he's dead, he's an angel now.

5. "Oh, sev'n long years made a great alt'ration,
     and sev'n more years I will wait for him,
   But if he's alive, oh, I love him dearly,
     and if he's dead, he's an angel now."

6. He pulled his hand out of his pocket,
     she spied a ring on his finger small,
   Saying, "I'm your poor and lonely sailor,
     who have just returned for to marry thee."

7. He picked her up and gave her kisses,
     and gave her kisses both one, two, three,
   Saying, "I'm your poor and lonely sailor,
     who have just returned from the raging sea."

8. Those lovely couple they got married,
     contented lives they did live together,
   Contented lives they did live together;
     and that's the end of 'My Sailor Boy.'

Grace Darling

Text: Frances Repetto (in writing).
Tune: Frances Repetto.
1/1-2 should probably read:
>'Twas on a storm-swept lighthouse,
>>there dwelt an English maid,
>Pure as the air around her,
>>of danger ne'er afraid.

2/2 should probably read:
>Between them and destruction
>>were the planks of the frail boat.
>It is possible that stanzas 2 and 3 should be in reversed order.

1. It was on a storm stone lighthouse,
            there dwelt an English maid,
   Pure as the air around her,
            of danger never feared.
   One morning just at daybreak
            a storm-tossed wreck spied she;
   Although to try seem' madness,
            "I'll save that crew!" cried she.
      She pulled away o'er the raging sea,
            all o'er the waters blue.
      "Help! Help!" you could hear the cry
            of the shipwreck' crew.
      Oh, Grace had an English heart,
            and the raging storm she braved;
      She pulled away o'er the dashing spray,
            and the crew she saved.

2. Then first one prayer to Heaven,
            and then they were afloat.
   Between them and destruction
            and the planks of the frail boat.
   Then cried the maiden's father,
            "Return and do not weep!"
   But up spoke brave Grace Darling,
            "Alone I'll face the deep."
      She pulled away o'er the raging sea, *etc.*

3. Then to the rocks were clinging
            a crew of nine all told;
   Between them and destruction
            the sea like mountains roll'.
   Cried Grace, "Come help me, father,
            we'll save that crew!" cried she.
   "It's madness," cried her father,
            "to face that angry sea!"
      She pulled away o'er the raging sea, *etc.*

4. Then bravely o'er the billows
            they did reach the wreck at length,
   And saved the storm-tossed sailors;
            in Heaven alone there's strength.
   Go tell the wide world over

What English pluck can do,
And sing of brave Grace Darling,
        who nobly saved the crew.
She pulled away o'er the raging sea,
        all o'er the waters blue.
"Help! Help!" you could hear the cry
        of the shipwreck' crew.
Oh, Grace had an English heart,
        and the raging storm she braved;
She pulled away o'er the dashing spray,
        and the crew she saved.

When I Was Young and in My Prime"

Text: Frances Repetto (in writing).

1. When I was young and in my prime,
        The sea I had to roam,
    My friends in one did me combine
        To part me from my love.

2. And now from Belfast we set sail,
        As you shall shortly hear,
    And down the dock we sailed away
        With a sweet and pleasant gale.

3. Bidding farewell to the Shamrock shore
        And the bonnie bonnie banks of the band,
    And a charming girl that I adore,
        She's my charming lovely Ann.

4. On the third night at eleven o'clock
        We got a dreadful shock;
    Our vessel she dashed with all her might
        Against a solid rock.

5. And there we laid till the break of day —
        Describe her fate who can —
    And this I to myself did say:
        "Adieu, sweet lovely Ann!"

6. As soon as we got one glimpse of light,
   Our boats we did employ,
   Towards the shore we took our flight,
   No danger then was nigh.

7. For Providence to us prove' kind,
   Whose name we do adore,
   And not one soul was left behind,
   But we all got saved on shore.

8. Farewell on to America
   And the rocks of rattle band.
   No more I'll from my country stray
   To cross the raging Main.

9. I'll go and see my bonnie girl
   Down by the river band,
   And all my days with her I'll spend,
   She's my charming lovely Ann.

The Sailor Boy

Text and tune: Alice Swain (Glass) from Fred Swain.
Cf. "The Sailor Boy" (Doerflinger, 1951, p. 164); "The Faithful Sailor Boy" (Laws, 1957, p. 147).
Norwegian version: "En sjøgutt nedpaa kaien stod."

One dark and stor - my win - ter's night, the snow fell on the
Chorus "Fare-well, my love, my own true love, this par - ting gives me

ground, A sai - lor boy stood on the quay, for his ship were out-ward
pain, You'll be my hope and gui-ding star till I re-turn a -

bound; His sweet-heart stan-ding by his side shed ma - 'ny a si - lent
gain. My thoughts will ev - er be of you when storms are ra - ging

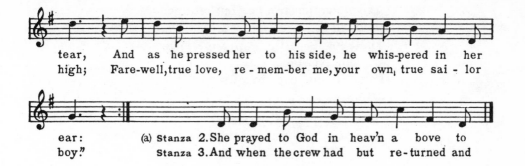

tear,   And as he pressed her   to   his side, he whis-pered in   her
high;   Fare-well, true love,   re - mem-ber me, your   own, true sai - lor

ear: (a) Stanza 2. She prayed to God in heav'n a   bove   to
boy?"   Stanza 3. And when the crew had   but   re-turned and

1. One dark and stormy winter's night,
        the snow fell on the ground,
    A sailor boy stood on the quay,
        for his ship were outward bound;
    His sweetheart standing by his side
        shed many a silent tear,
    And as he pressed her to his side,
        he whispered in her ear:
    Farewell, my love, my own true love,
        this parting gives me pain,
    You'll be my hope and guiding star
        till I return again.
    My thoughts will ever be of you
        when storms are raging high;
    Farewell, true love, remember me,
        your own true sailor boy.

2. Now in that gale that ship set sail,
        his love was standing by;
    She watched the vessel out of sight
        till tears bedim' her eyes.
    She prayed to God in heav'n above
        to guide her sailor on;
    Those loving parting words that night
        re-echo o'er the Main:
    Farewell, my love, my own true love, *etc.*

3. It's hard to say that ship returned
        without her sailor boy;
    He must have died well on the sea,
        for the flag were half mast high.

And when the crew had but returned
and tell her love was dead,
Those loving parting words that night
re-echo o'er the Main:
Farewell, my love, my own true love, *etc.*

A Light in the Window

Text: Fred Swain
Tune: Alice Swain (Glass).
Norwegian version: "Det lyser i et vindu."

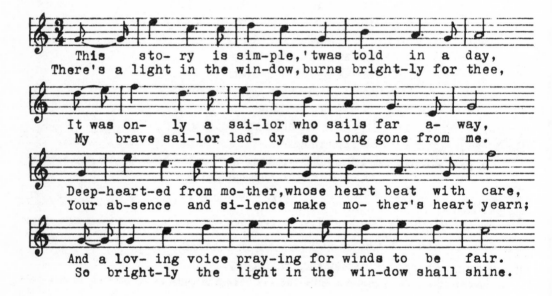

1. This story is simple, 'twas told in a day,
   It was only a sailor who sails far away,
   Deephearted from mother, whose heart beat with care,
   And a loving voice praying for winds to be fair.
   There's a light in the window, burns brightly for thee,
   My brave sailor laddy so long gone from me.
   Your absence and silence make mother's heart yearn.
   So brightly the light in the window shall shine.

2. At last the long years came and went as a dream,
   Some stories of wreckage came from the Gulf. Stream.
   So brightly the light in the window it gleams,
   Intended for him who lives only in dreams.
   There's a light in the window, *etc.*

3. —Step to the door-step — no answer there came.
   —Step to the window and peeps through the pane.
   —Mother lies dead, but the light brightly shine,
   She still keep it burning for one far from home.
   There's a light in the window, burns brightly for thee,
   My brave sailor laddy so long gone from me.
   Your absence and silence make mother's heart yearn.
   So brightly the light in the window shall shine.

A Poor Anxious Woman

Text and tune: Fred Swain.

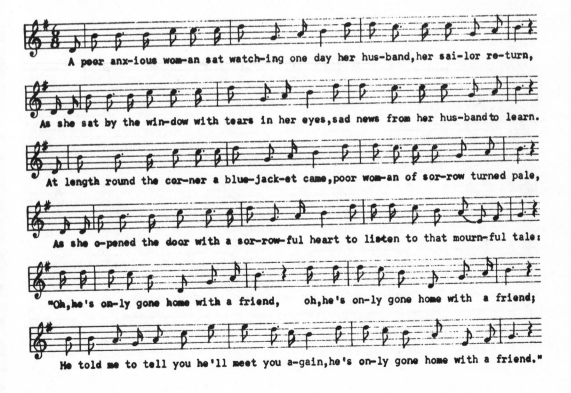

A poor anx-ious wom-an sat watch-ing one day her hus-band, her sai-lor re-turn,

As she sat by the win-dow with tears in her eyes, sad news from her hus-band to learn.

At length round the cor-ner a blue-jack-et came, poor wom-an of sor-row turned pale,

As she o-pened the door with a sor-row-ful heart to listen to that mourn-ful tale:

"Oh, he's on-ly gone home with a friend, oh, he's on-ly gone home with a friend;

He told me to tell you he'll meet you a-gain, he's on-ly gone home with a friend."

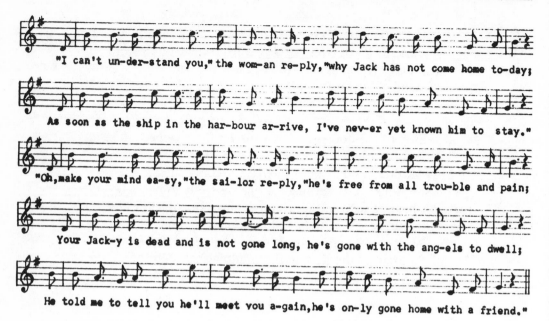

"I can't un-der-stand you," the wom-an re-ply, "why Jack has not come home to-day;

As soon as the ship in the har-bour ar-rive, I've nev-er yet known him to stay."

"Oh, make your mind ea-sy," the sai-lor re-ply, "he's free from all trou-ble and pain;

Your Jack-y is dead and is not gone long, he's gone with the ang-els to dwell;

He told me to tell you he'll meet you a-gain, he's on-ly gone home with a friend."

The Ship That Never Returned

Text: A, Alice Swain (Glass);
    B, Agnes Rogers (in writing).
Tune: Alice Swain (Glass).
Cf. Laws, 1964, p. 174.

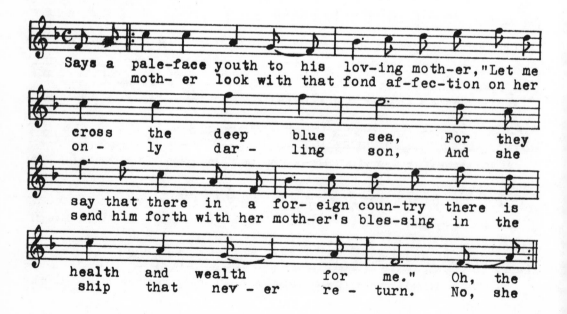

Says a pale-face youth to his lov-ing moth-er, "Let me
moth- er   look with that fond af-fec-tion on her

cross   the   deep   blue   sea,   For   they
on - ly   dar - ling   son,   And   she

say that there in a for-eign coun-try there is
send him forth with her moth-er's bles-sing in the

health   and   wealth   for   me."   Oh, the
ship   that   nev - er   re - turn.   No, she

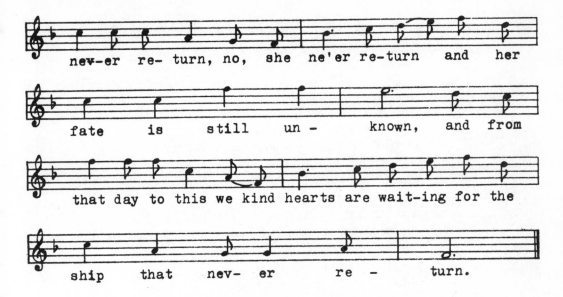

nev-er re- turn, no, she ne'er re-turn and her

fate is still un - known, and from

that day to this we kind hearts are wait-ing for the

ship that nev- er re - turn.

A

1. Says a pale face youth to his loving mother,
   "Let me cross the deep blue sea,
   For they say that there in a foreign country
   there is health and wealth for me."
   Oh, the mother look with that fond affection
   on her only darling son,
   And she send him forth with her mother's blessing
   in the ship that never return.
   No, she never return, no, she ne'er return,
   and her fate is still unknown,
   And from that day to this we kind hearts are waiting
   for the ship that never return.

2. "Only one more trip," says the gallant sailor
   as he kissed his fond young wife,
   "Only one more bag of that golden treasure,
   and we'll settle down for life;
   Yes, we'll settle down in a cosy corner
   with the wealth that we have got."
   But she little know 'twas a solemn parting
   of the ship that never return.
   No, she never return, no, sne ne'er return,
   and her fate is still unknown,

And from that day to this we kind hearts are waiting
  for the ship that never return.

                    B
1. Said a pale face youth to his loving mother,
      "Let me cross the deep blue sea,
    For they say that there in a foren country
      there is health and wealth for me."
    The mother looked with fond affection
      on her only darling son,
    And she sent him forth with a mother's blessing
      in the ship that never returned.
      No, she never returned, no, she never returned,
        and her faith is still unknown;
      But from that to this kind hearts are waiting
        for the ship that never returned.

2. "Only one more trip," said the gallant sailor
      as he kissed his fond young wife,
    "Only one more bag of that golden treasure,
      and we'll settle down for life;
    Yes, we'll settle down in a cosy corner
      with the wealth that we have got."
    But she little knew 'twas a solom parting,
      for the ship she never returned.
      No, she never returned, no, she never returned,
        and her faith is still unknown;
      But from that day to this kind hearts are asking
        for the ship that never returned.

Adieu, Sweet Lovely Nancy

Text and tune: Alice Swain (Glass).

1. Adieu, sweet lovely Nancy,
     ten thousand times adieu;
   I am going across the ocean
     to seek for something new.
   Come and change your ring with me, my dear,
     come and change your ring with me,
   And that will be a token
     while I am on the sea.

2. . . . .
     . . . .
     . . . .
     . . . .
     While I am on the sea, my dear,
       you may know not where I am,
     But the letters I will write to you
       from every foreign land.

3. . . . .
     . . . .
     . . . .
     . . . .
     The secret of my heart, my dear,
       and the best of my good will;
     Oh, let my body, o, be where it will,
       my heart are with you still.

4. See how those storms are raging,
       see how they are coming on,
     And we all jolly sailors
       are fighting for the Crown;
     Our officers command us,
       and them we must obey
     Until the very moment
       till we are cast away.

5. And now the storm is all over,
       and we all safe on shore;
     We will drink to our wives and sweethearts
       and the girls that we adore,
     We will call for liquor merrily
       and spend our money free,
     And when our money, o, it is all gone,
       we will boldly go to sea.

Ranso

Text: Old Sam Swain
Cf:"Reuben Ranzo" (Linscott, 1939, p. 144 ff.; Doerflinger, 1951, p. 23 ff.;
Mackenzie, 1963, p. 265).

1. Ranso was a mighty man,
   Ranso — Ranso!
   Ranso was a mighty man.

2. He shipped on board a whaler,
   All along with Captain Taylor.

3. Ranso was a bad old sailor,
   Ranso was a bad old sailor.

4. He sent him up in the forecastle,
   He sent him up in the forecastle.

5. He called him up from down below,
   And is up aloft that you must go.

6. He called him down from up aloft,
   He called him down from up aloft.

7. Ranso 'came a good old man,
   Ranso 'came a good old sailor.

8. He called him af' to the cabin,
   And he gave him nine and thirty lashes.

9. And he called him down in the cabin,
   He gave him wine and brandy.

10. Oh, Ranso 'came a handy man,
    Ranso — Ranso!
    Oh, he married a captain's daughter.

Whiskey — Johnny

Text and tune: Old Sam Swain.
The order of the lines might vary; the one given here is the one presented when the
shanty was recorded.
Cf. Linscott, 1939, p. 151 f.; Doerflinger, 1951, p. 15f; Mackenzie 1963, p. 271 f.

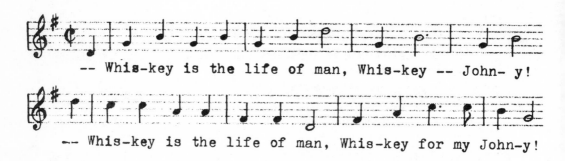

-- Whis-key is the life of man, Whis-key -- John- y!

-- Whis-key is the life of man, Whis-key for my John-y!

1. In London City you'll see me here,
    Whiskey — Johnny!
   In London City you'll see me here.
    Whiskey for my Johnny!

2. I met with a girl was free and young. *(twice)*

3. Whiskey is the life of man. *(twice)*

4. Whiskey gave me a broken head. *(twice)*

5. Whiskey gave me a broken nose. *(twice)*

6. She went to bed, and so did I. *(twice)*

7. She stole my gold watch and silver chain,
   She stole my gold watch and silver snuffbox.

8. Whiskey killed my old grand-dad,
    Whiskey — Johnny!
   Whiskey killed my old grand-dad.
    Whiskey for my Johnny!

Come All Ye Bold Seamen

Text and tune: Old Sam Swain ("from the shipping time of Thomas H. Swain").

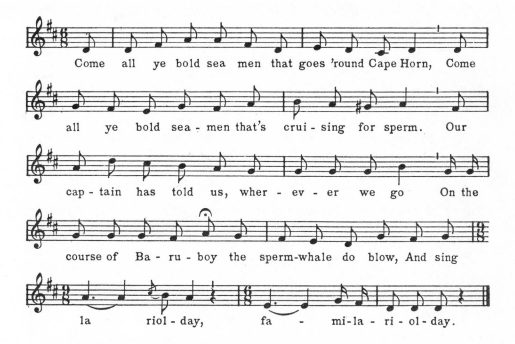

1. Come all ye bold seamen that goes 'round Cape Horn,
   Come all ye bold seamen that's cruising for sperm.
   Our captain 'as told us, wherever we go
   On the course of Baruboy the sperm whale do blow,
   And sing la-riol-day, fa-mila-ri-ol-day.

2. Early next morning before the sun rose,
   Our man from the masthead cried out, "There she blows!"
   Our captain bin af' and answered him so:
   "Two points to the lee bow about three mile off,"
   And sing la-riol-day, fa-mila-ri-ol-day.

3. See our tublines well clear and hines* were sharp;
   Swaw up your boat, boys, and jump in, bold crew!
   Our boatsteerer struck him, and the whale he went down,
   Our captain hove up for a line to bend on,
   And sing la-riol-day, fa-mila-ri-ol-day.

4. We've towed him alongside with many a shout,
   To-day we'll cut in, and to-morrow we'll try out.
   Oh, now he's tried out, boys, and likewise towed down,
   He's better to us than five hundred pound,
   And sing la-riol-day, fa-mila-ri-ol-day.

  * irons (?)

THE BALLAD TRADITION

Maria Martini

Text: A, Frances Repetto (in writing);
      B, Lily Green (written down by Agnes Rogers).
Tune: Arthur Repetto.
The tune is in a pentatonic Dorian mode (see p.   n.).
Cf. "The Gosport Tragedy" (Leach, 1955, p. 698 ff.); "The Lexington Murder"
ibid., p. 785ff.); "Naomi Wise" or "Omie Wise" *(ibid.,* p. 793ff. Lomax, 1960, p.
268); "Rose Connelly" (Lomax, 1960, p. 267); "Tom Dula" *(ibid.,* p. 269). For
further references, see Laws, 1957, p. 267 ff. Mackenzie, 1963, p. 293.
In version A, 3/3, Frances Repetto wrote "damsel" but sang "innocent."

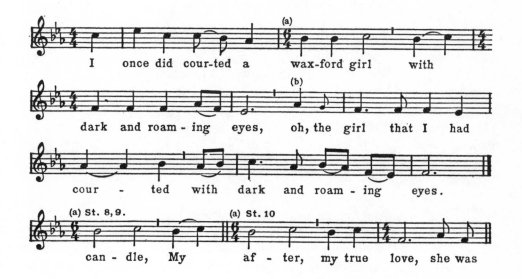

sil-ly young men, Take   un - til I came to a   ri - ver-side

I   gave him an an - swer that I   thought fit .

A

1. I once did courted a waxford girl
    with dark and roaming eyes,
   Oh, the girl that I had courted
    with dark and roaming eyes.

2. I went down to her father's house
    about eight o'clock at night,
   And asked her for to take a walk
    across King William's Town.

3. I picked a stick from the riverside,
    and I tap her on the head,
   While the blood from this young damsel
    went a-streaming on the ground.

4. Down on her bending knees she fell
    and loud for mercy call,
   Saying, "John, my dear, don't murder me,
    for I'm not fit to die."

5. I take hold of her curly locks,
    and I drag her cross the field,
   Until I came to a riverside,
    and there I threwed her in.

6. And I going down to my master's house
    about ten o'clock at night,
   My master being out of bed,
    a-striking of the 'larm.

7. My master he asked me a request,
    what had soil my hands and clothes;

I gave him an answer that I thought fit:
"I'm a-bleeding at the nose."

8. I take hold of the candle,
   myself I lights to bed,
While the blazing flames of torment
   around my eyes did shine.

9. I take hold of the candle,
   myself I lights to bed,
But all that blessed long night
   my true love she laid dead.

10. Not less than three days after,
    my true love she was found
A-floating on a river
    close by her sister's door.

11. Then I was taken on suspicion
    and into prison was cast
For the murder of my own true love,
    so I must die at last.

12. Come all you young and silly young men,
    Take warning unto this,
And never do no murder
    for to be hung like me.

B

1. I have courted a waxen girl
   with the dark and roving eye,
The girl that I have courted
   with the dark and roving eye.

2. He came to my master's house
   at eight o'clock one night,
And asked me to take a walk
   through green and mellow fields.

3. And as we were a-walking,
   he stopped to talk a while,
And he pulled a stick out of the hedge

and tapped her on the side.

4. Then on her bendening knees she fell,
     crying, "Mercy, Lord, on me!"
   Saying, "John, my dear, don't murder me,
     for I'm not fit to die."

5. The blood from this young damsel's side
     come streaming on the ground,
   Oh, the blood from this young damsel's side
     come a-streaming on the ground.

6. He took her by the curly head
     and drew her over the field
   Till he came by the riverside,
     and there he threw her in.

7. My master being out of bed
     and striking of a light,
   My master being out of bed
     at ten o'clock at night.

8. He asked me and questioned me,
     what soiled my hand and clothes,
   I gave him an answer I thought fit:
     "I am bleeding from the nose."

9. And all the blessed long night through
     the flames round my head,
   And all the blessed long night through
     the burning flames round my head.

10. Nine days after, this young damsel's body
     came a-floating down,
   Came a-floating pass her sister's house,
     and that is the way she was found.

11. They took me up on (. . . ?),
     and into prison I was cast,
   And there I stayed till I was tried
     and now to be hung at last.

12. Come all you faithful sailor boys,
    come take a warning from me,
    And don't you do no murder,
    and now to be hung at last.

The Lowlands Low
or
The Golden Vanity

Text and tune: Old Sam Swain.
Cf. Child, No. 286; Coffin, 1950, p. 153 ff.; "The Merry Golden Tree" (Wells,
1950, p. 53f.); "The Sweet Trinity" or "The Golden Vanity" (Leach, 1955, p.
667 ff., Lomax, 1960, p. 191 f.); etc. A New England version of this song, ' The
Gallant Victory" or "Lowlands Low" (Linscott, 1939, p. 136 f.), has a closely
related tune.

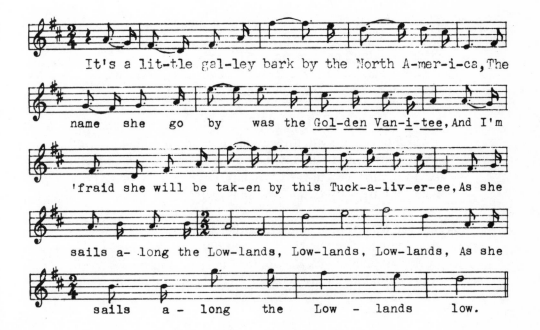

1. It's a little galley bark by the North America,
   The name she go by was the *Golden Vanity,*
   And I'm 'fraid she will be taken by this Tuckaliveree.
   As she sails along the Lowlands, Lowlands, Lowlands,
   As she sails along the Lowlands low.

2. And up spoke the boy, the pretty cabin boy,
   "Captain, what you'll give me if the vessel I destroy?"
   "I will give you gold and silver and my daughter for your bride
   If you'll sink her in the Lowlands, Lowlands, Lowlands,
   If you'll sink her in the Lowlands low."

3. The boy bent his cashpere and overboard he went,
   He swam till he swam till this Tuckaliveree,
   And he swam till he swam till this Tuckaliveree
   As she sails along the Lowlands, Lowlands, Lowlands,
   As she sails along the Lowlands low.

4. And two holes he bored once, and two holes he bored twice,
   While some were playing cards and the other was shaking dice,
   While some were playing cards and the water was floating in,
   They were sinking in the Lowlands, Lowlands, Lowlands,
   They were sinking in the Lowlands low.

5. Then he swam till he swam to his own ship again,
   Says, "Captain, pick me up, for I'm sinking in the sea,"
   Says, "Captain, pick me up, for I'm sinking in the sea,
   And I'm sinking in the Lowlands, Lowlands, Lowlands,
   And I'm sinking in the Lowlands low."

6. Says the captain, "Pick you up is a thing I never do.
   I will shoot you, I will drown you, I will do it with good will,
   I will shoot you, I will drown you, I will do it with good will,
   And I'll burry you in the Lowlands, Lowlands, Lowlands,
   And I'll burry you in the Lowlands low."

7. He swan till he swam all on the other side,
   And there he saw his shipmate, and bitter he did cry;
   Says, "Shipmate, pick me up, for I'm sinking in the sea,
   And I'm sinking in the Lowlands, Lowlands, Lowlands,
   And I'm sinking in the Lowlands low."

8. And the shipmate pick him up, and on the deck he died;
    He rolled him in his hammock and launched him o'er the side,
    He rolled him in his hammock and launched him o'er the side,
    And he burried him in the Lowlands, Lowlands, Lowlands,
    And he burried him in the Lowlands low.

The Turkish Lady

Text: Lily Green (written down by Agnes Rogers).
Tune: Alice Swain (Glass).
Cf. "Young Beichan" (Child, No. 53; Leach, 1955, p. 170 ff.); "The Turkish Lady
(Leach, p. 173 f.); Coffin, 1950, p. 63 ff.; Laws, 1957, p. 238. A practically
identical variant from Nova Scotia has been published by Mackenzie, 1963, p. 66 f.
3/2, according to Mary Swain, should read:
        As we were sailing far away.
11/3 should probably read:
        Who was from chain and bondage free.

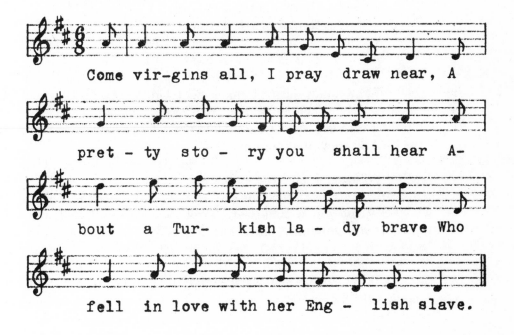

1. Come virgins all, I pray draw near,
   A pretty story you shall hear
   About a Turkish lady brave,
   Who fell in love with her English slave.

2. Now sit you down and listen a while,
   And hear my story, it was for a while
   It was my fortune for to be
   A slave unto a rich lady.

3. A merchant ship at Bristol lay,
   As we were sailing far over the sea,
   A Turkish rover took were we,
   And all of us made slaves to be.

4. They bound us down in iron strong,
   They whipped and lashed us all along,
   No tongue can tell, I am certainly sure,
   What we poor wreched souls did endure.

5. She dressed herself in rich array
   And went to view her slaves one day,
   And hearing a moan a young man made,
   She went to him and thus did say:

6. "What countryman, young man, are you?"
   "I am an Englishman, that true."
   "I wish you were a Turk," said she,
   "I'd ease you of your misery."

7. "I'd own myself to be your wife,
   For I do love you as my life;
   I'd ease you of your slavish work
   If you consent to turn a Turk."

8. – "Oh no, no, madam," said he,
   "Your consent slave, dear madam, I'll be,
   For I would sooner be burnt at the stake
   Before I would my God forsake."

9. This lady to her chamber went
   And spent the night in discont(ent);

Little Cupid with his piercing dart
Had deeply wounded her to the heart.

10. She was resolved the very next day
    To ease him of his slavery work,
    And owned herself to be his wife,
    For she did love him as her life.

11. For she has turned a Christian brave,
    And she is wed to her own slave,
    Who was in chain and bondage free;
    So this you see what love can do.

12. She dressed herself in rich array,
    And with this young man sailed away,
    And to her parents bid adieu;
    So this you see what love can do.

The Old Miser

Text and tune: Arthur Repetto.
The influence from the Tristan dialect seems to be particularly strong in this song.

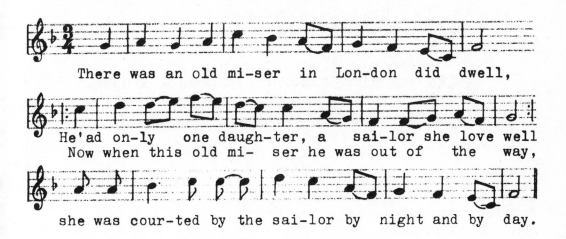

There was an old mi-ser in Lon-don did dwell,

He'ad on-ly one daugh-ter, a sai-lor she love well
Now when this old mi- ser he was out of the way,

she was cour-ted by the sai-lor by night and by day.

1. There was an old miser in London did dwell,
   He 'ad only one daughter, a sailor she love well;

Now when this old miser he was out of the way,
She was courted by the sailor by night and by day.

2. Now when this old miser he did heard of this news,
   Straight 'way to the captain this old miser he did go,
   Saying, "Captain, bold captain, good news I have got to tell,
   I 'as got a young sailor as a transport to sell."

3. Then up spoke the captain, "And you bring him to me,
   and I'll send him a-sailing far over the sea,
   . . . .
   and he'll ne'er return to England for to court her again."

4. Now soon this young lady she did heard of this news,
   Straight 'way to the captain this young lady she did go,
   Crying, "Captain, bold captain, sad news I have got to tell,
   You 'as got my young sailor as a transport to sell."

5. It was down on the deck this young lady she did stood,
   And 'twas down on the main deck she throwed handfuls of gold,
   Crying, "Captain, bold captain, all this I'll give to you
   If you give me back my sailor, he's my rights and my due."

6. "Oh no, fairest lady, that's a thing I ne'er can do,
   For your father has sold him as a transport to me,
   And I'll send him a-sailing far over the sea,
   And he'll ne'er return to England for to court you again."

7. "So is bad luck to my old father wheresoever he may be,
   And I'm thinking in my own heart that he's quite wrong with me;
   I'll go back to my cottage, and I'll lay myself down,
   And I'll mourn there for my sailor, he's my rights and my due."

The Butcher Boy

Text: Lily Green (written down by Agnes Rogers).
Tune: Alice Swain (Glass).
Cf. "I Wish in Vain" (Korson, 1949, p. 48f.); "The Butcher Boy" (Linscott, 1939, p. 179 ff.; Leach, 1955, p. 737 f.); Laws, 1957, p. 260; Mackenzie, 1963, p. 157 ff. For the tune, cf. "Henry Dear" (p. 49).

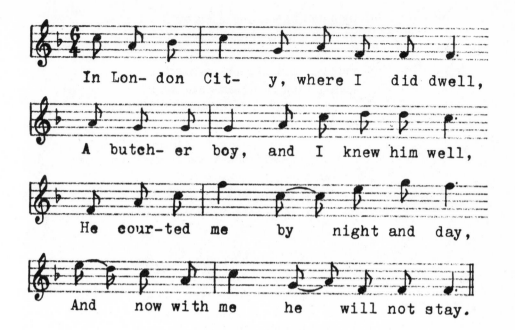

In Lon- don Cit- y, where I did dwell,

A butch- er boy, and I knew him well,

He cour-ted me by night and day,

And now with me he will not stay.

1. In London City, where I did dwell,
   A butcher boy, and I knew him well,
   He courted me by night and day,
   And now with me he will not stay.

2. He takes another girl upon his knee,
   And he tells to her what he don't tell me;
   He takes another girl upon his knee,
   Now, don't you think that it's grief to me.

3. It's grief to me, and I'll tell you why,
   Because she has more gold than I;
   Her gold will melt and her silver fly,
   In time of need she be as poor as I.

4. When her father came home from work.
   He asked his wife where his daughter was;
   He rushed upstairs and the door he broke,
   And he found her hanging onto a rope.

5. He took a knife and he cut her down,
   And in her bosom these few lines he found:

"Oh, what a foolish young maid was I
To hang myself for a butcher boy.

6. – "Dig my grave, dig it wide and deep,
Put a marble stone at my head and feet,
And on my breast put a turtle dove,
That the world may know that I died for love.

7. "I died for love, as you plainly see,
I died for love, as you plainly see,
For loving of a butcher boy
That never loved me."

The Rich Merchant

Text: A, Mary Swain;
     B, Lily Green (written down by Agnes Rogers).
Tune: Mary Swain.
Cf. "The Highway Robber" (Greenleaf, 1933, p. 47f.), and "The Crafty Farmer"
(Child, No. 283; Leach, 1955, p. 662 ff.); Laws, 1957, p. 73 ff., p. 165 f. Coffin,
1950, p. 151 f.

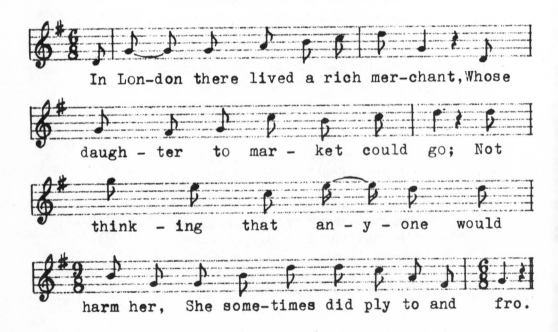

A

1. In London there lived a rich merchant,
   Whose daughter to market could go.
   Not thinking that anyone would harm her,
   She sometimes did ply to and fro.

2. One day as she was returning,
   A highwayman met her that way;
   The highway being so very well a-mounted,
   He soon did oblige her to stay.

3. 'Twas down he did strip this fair damsel,
   And he gave her the bridle to hold,
   And there she stood shivering and shaking
   As if she should perish with cold.

4. She whipped her left foot in the stirrup,
   And over the saddle rode she,
   With the highwayman's horse went a-galloping,
   Five miles in ten minutes rode she.

5. The highwayman soon followed after,
   He ran and he puffed and he blew,
   He ran, but he could not come near her,
   Saying, "Damsel, I'll give you your clothes."

6. "My clothes, kind Sir, I don't want them,
   You can keep them yourself if you please."
   He ran, but he could not come nigh her,
   His boots they did hamp on his knees.

7. She let him through hills and through valleys
   Till she came to a place she know well;
   There she left him a parcel of farthings,
   The worth of five shillings to tell.

8. "Oh, what has befell you, dear daughter,
   That you have been staying so long?"
   "Oh, nothing has befell me, dear father,
   I'm sure I've received no wrong!"

9. Then down she took the portmaneteau,
   And in it the money was found,
   It was all in good gold and silver
   To the amount of five hundred pound.

10. "Oh, five hundred pound, my dear daughter,
    And five hundred I'll give you more;
    It'll do very well to relieve you
    and keep the cold wind from your door."

B

1. In London there lived a rich merchant,
   Whose daughter to market would go;
   Not thinking that any one would harm her,
   She often times went to and fro.

2. One day as she was a-walking,
   A highwayman met her that way;
   The highway being very well mounted,
   He soon did oblige her to stay.

3. And there he did strip this fair damsel,
   And he gave her the bridle to hold,
   And there she stood shivering and shaking,
   As though she would perish with cold.

4. She stepped her left foot in the stirrup
   And over the saddle did stride,
   With the highwayman's horse went a-galloping,
   Five miles in ten minutes did ride.

5. The highwayman soon followed after,
   He ran and he puffed and he blew,
   He ran, but he could not come near her,
   Crying, "Damsel, I'll give you your clothes."

6. "My clothes, kind Sir, I don't want them,
   You can keep them yourself if you please."
   He ran, but he could not come nigh her,
   His boots they did cramp up his knees.

7. Her mother been very much a-frightened,
   It bein' just twelve by the clock,
   Her father been very much a-frightened
   To see her come home in a smock.

8. "Oh, what has befell you, dear daughter,
   That you have been staying so long?"
   "Oh, nothing has befell me, dear father,
   And I have received no wrong."

9. Then down she took the portmounter,
   And in it the money was found,
   Amounting in good gold and silver
   The sum of five thousand pound.

10. "Oh, five thousand pound, my dear daughter,
    And five thousand I'll give you more;
    It will do very well to relieve you
    And keep the cold wind from your door,
    It will do very well to relieve you
    And keep the cold wind from your door."

There Was a Wealthy Farmer
or
The Girl I Left Behind

Text: A, Frances Repetto;
      B, Henry Green.
Tune: Henry Green.
The tune is built on an hexatonic scale with unsettled (or inflected) 4th and with an unusually large fifth interval, comprising a major 3rd. Conventionally speaking, it "lacks the 6th." On the latter point it differs markedly from the regular traditional ballad modes. It could probably still be described as either Lydian or Ionian or perhaps, in Bronson's terms (1946; 1959/62, vol. 2, p. xii), as Ly/I −6. It is a plagal tune, moving within the octave between two dominants, and it ends on the lower dominant. This as well as the over-augmented interval immediately above the dominant gives a peculiar emphasis to that tone which is evident throughout the tune.
Cf. "The Girl I Left Behind," rendered by Lomax (1960, p. 318f.) in a pentatonic mode of definite AEolian quality. See also Laws, 1957, p. 248.

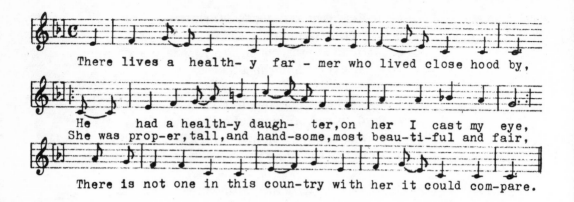

There lives a health- y far - mer who lived close hood by,

He had a health-y daugh- ter, on her I cast my eye,
She was prop-er, tall, and hand-some, most beau-ti-ful and fair,

There is not one in this coun-try with her it could com-pare.

A

1. There was a wealthy farmer who lived close hardly by,
   He had a handsome daughter, on her I cast my eye;
   She was proper, tall, and handsome, most beautiful and fair,
   There is not one in this country with her I can compare.

2. I ask if she be willing till I recrossed the sea,
   . . . .
   She said she would be true to me if I proved true in kind;
   Then we shook hands and parted with the girl I left behind.

3. Now we sail out from the island, to New York we were bound,
   Steering our course to America to view that blooming town,
   With money and trade in plenty, and the girls to me proved true
   That the sweetest object of my heart was the girl I left behind.

4. One evening as I was done my work, I roam through Georgie Square,
   Where the mail-cart just arrived and the postboy met me there,
   And he handed to me a letter which cost me two hundred stern:
   The girl I left behind me, she got wed to another man.

5. I advanced a little farther, finding the news was true,
   I turned myself all round about, not knowing what to do,
   . . . .
   That the girl I left behind me, she got wed to another man.

6. If this you say to me be true, how can I believe the fare,
   For the very last night we parted was on that Book she swore,

The very last night we parted, she vow to me sincere
That she would wed with none but me, she vowed it o'er and o'er.

7. . . . .
. . . .
Till I became a rover bou(?), which grieve my heart full sore,
For to leave my own dear country and never see it any more.

8. One evening as I sit courting, "Don't grieve, my boy," said she,
"For I have money plenty to serve both you and me;
Your pockets will be loaded of gold and silver both
If you'll agree and marry me and say you'll roam no more."

9. . . . .
She was handsome Peggy Walker, she fell in love with me;
My pocket being empty I thought it in full time
To stay with her and think no more of the girl I left behind.

B
1. There lives a healthy farmer who lived close hood by,
He had a healthy daughter, on her I cast my eye;
She was proper, tall, and handsome, most beautiful and fair,
There is not one in this country with her it could compare.

2. I ask if she be willing till I had crossed the sea,
. . . .
She said she would be true with me if I proved true in turn;
Then we shook hands and parted as I left her behind.

3. Now we sail out from off the island, to New York we were bound,
Steering our course to America to view that blooming town,
With money and trade in plenty, and the girls to me proved true
That the sweetest object of my heart was the girl I left behind.

4. One evening as I was done my work, I roam through Georgie Square,
Where just the post-cart rises and the postboy met me near,
And he handed to me a letter which cost me a hundred stern:
The girl that I had left behind, she got wed with another man.

5. I went see her little father, find if the thing be true,
I turn myself right round abou', not knowing what to do,

Till I become a rover bou (?), which grieve my heart full shame
For to leave my own dear country and never for to see it again.

6. If this you say be true to me, how can I believe the fare,
   For the very last night we parted, on the Book she swear,
   . . . .
   That she would wed none one but me, she vowed it o'er and o'er.

7. There said a healthy lady, "Don't grieve, my boy, for shame,
   For money I got plenty to serve both me and you;
   Your pockets will be loaded of gold and silver both
   If you will come and stay with me and say you'll wrong no more."

                            Barv'ry Allen
                                 or
                           Barbara Allan

Text and tune: Alice Swain (Glass).
Of the numerous versions recorded and published of this extremely popular song, cf.
particularly "Bonny Barbara Allan" (Child, No. 84; Leach, 1955, p. 277 ff.; Tolman,
1916, p. 161f), "Barb'ry Ellen" (Linscott, 1939, p. 163 f.), and variants Nos. 3, 12,
21, 30, 36, 37, 43, 45, 50, 85, 91, 97, 127, 133, etc. in Bronson (1959/62, vol. II,
pp. 326-391). For the tune, cf. Bronson's variants Nos. 1-39, particularly No. 9.

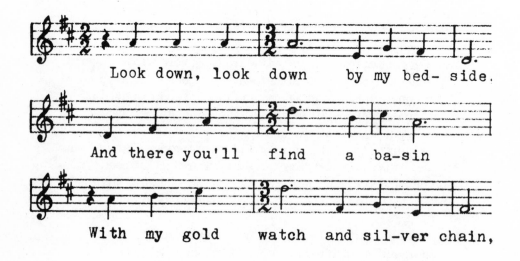

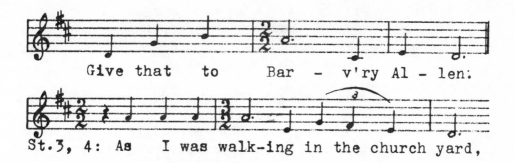

Alternative notation:

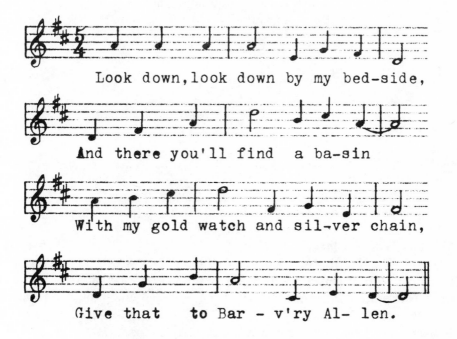

1. "Look down, look down by my bedside,
   And there you'll find a basin
   With my gold watch and silver chain,
   Give that to Barv'ry Allen.

2. "Look down, look down by my bedside,
   And there you'll find a towel
   With my gold watch and silver chain,
   Give that to Barv'ry Allen."

3. As I was walking in the church yard,
   I heard those bells a-tolling,
   And as they tolled, they seemed to say:
   "Cruel-hearted Barv'ry Allen!"

4. As I was walking in the church yard,
   I heard those bells a-tolling,
   And as they tolled, they seemed to say:
   "Young man, I think you're dying."

5. — "Dying, oh no, that ne'er can be!
   A kiss from you will cure me."
   "A kiss from me you ne'er shall get —
   Keep your poor heart from breaking!"

Yonder
or
Oh No, John

Text: A, Henry Green;
      B, Frances Repetto;
      C, Frances Repetto (stanzas 1-4, in writing); Mary Swain (stanza 5).
Tune: A/B, Henry Green, Frances Repetto;
      C, Alice Swain (Glass).
      Cf. "Oh, No, No, Sir, No"(Korson, 1949, p. 50 f.), which shows that there is a traditional connection between versions A and B on the one hand and version C on the other. Numerous other versions have been recorded and published from various parts of England and North America.
      Stanza 5 of version C is obviously a secondary addition. It was not included by either Frances Repetto or Alice Swain and was generally treated as a separate ditty.
      Alice Swain sang the refrain of version C:
                  No, John, no, John, *etc.*
      Versions A and B were rendered by Henry Green and Frances Repetto, respectively, in the same authentic Mixolydian mode:

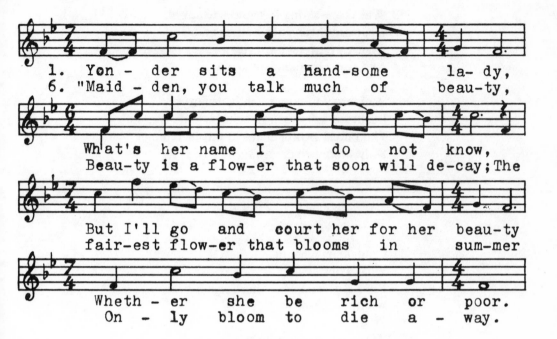

1. Yon - der sits   a   hand-some   la- dy,
6. "Maid - den, you   talk   much   of   beau-ty,

Wh'at's   her name   I   do   not   know,
Beau-ty is a flow-er that soon will de-cay;The

But I'll go   and   court her for her   beau-ty
fair-est flow-er that blooms   in   sum-mer

Wheth - er   she   be   rich   or   poor.
On - ly   bloom   to   die   a - way.

A

1. Yonder stand a handsome woman,
   What's her name I do not know,
   But I'll go and court her for her beauty
   Whether she be rich or no.

2. "Maiden, I am coming for to court you,
   If you' favour I can gain;
   But you kindly incontain* me,
   P'rhaps that I may come back again."

3. "You may go home, kind Sir, you're welcome,
   P'rhaps your face I'll never see more,
   But all I want is a handsome young man,
   Whether he be rich or poor."

4. "Maiden, I got gold and silver,
   Maiden, I got houses and land,
   Maiden, I got rings and jewelry,
   All shall be at your command."

* Apparently corrupted from 'entertain.'

5. "What care I for your gold and silver,
   What care I for your houses and land,
   What care I for your rings and jewelry,
   All I want is a handsome man."

6. "Maiden, you talk much of beauty,
   Beauty is a flower that soon will decay;
   The fairest flower that blooms in summer
   Only bloom to die away."

B

1. Yonder sits a handsome lady,
   What's her name I do not know,
   But I'll go and court her for her beauty
   Whether she be rich or poor.

2. "Maiden, I have come to court you,
   If your favour I can gain;
   But you kindly incontain me,
   P'rhaps I may come back again.

3. "Maiden, I got gold and silver,
   Maiden, I got houses and land,
   Maiden, I got rings and jewelry,
   All shall be at your command."

4. "What care I for your gold and silver,
   What care I for your houses and land,
   What care I for your rings and jewelry,
   All I want is a handsome man.

5. "You may go home, kind Sir, you're welcome,
   P'rhaps your face I'll never see more,
   But all I want is a handsome young man,
   Whether he be rich or poor."

6. "Maiden, you talk much of beauty,
   Beauty is a thing that soon will decay;

The fairest flower that blooms in summer
Only bloom to die away."

No, Sir
or
Lady Dear

"Tell me one thing, tell me tru-ly, tell me why you scorn me so, Tell me why, when asked a ques-tion, you will al - ways an - swer no: No, Sir, no, Sir, no, Sir, no, Sir, no, Sir, no."

1. "Tell me one thing, tell me truly,
      tell me why you scorn me so,
   Tell me why, when asked a question,
      you will always answer no:
         No, Sir, no, Sir,
            no, Sir, no, Sir, no, Sir, no."

2. "My father was a Spanish merchant,
    and before he went to sea,
He told me to be sure and answer
    no to all you said to me:
        No, Sir, no, Sir,
          no, Sir, no, Sir, no, Sir, no."

3. "If when walking in the garden,
    plucking flowers all wet with dew,
Oh, tell me, would you be offended
    if I walk and talk with you?"
        "No, Sir, no, Sir,
          no, Sir, no, Sir, no, Sir, no."

4. "If when walking in the garden,
    and I should ask you to be mine,
And should tell you that I love you,
    would you then my heart decline?"
        "No, Sir, no, Sir,
          no, Sir, no, Sir, no, Sir, no."

5. "Lady dear, let me tie your garter
    just one inch above your knee;
If my hand should slip 'little higher,'
    would you think it rude of me?"
        "No, Sir, no, Sir,
          no, Sir, no, Sir, no, Sir, no."

MISCELLANEA

Jealousy

Text: Lily Green (written down by Agnes Rogers).
Tune: Alice Swain (Glass).

   Cf. "Oxford City," Laws, 1957, p. 263. Alice Swain sang a slightly different text version of stanzas 1 and 4:

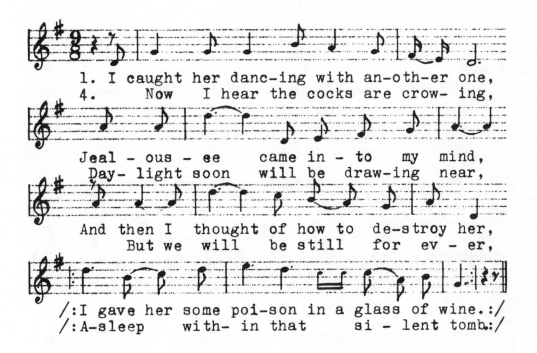

1. I caught her dancing with another one,
   Jealousy came into my mind,
   And then I thought for to destroy her,
   /:I gave her some poison in a glass of wine.:/

2. First she smiled and then she fainted,
   "Pick me up, love, carry me home,
   For it was poison that you gave to me
   /:To take my sweet young life away.":/

3. "If it was poison that I gave to you,
   I will drink, love, then we shall see;
   Then in each other's arms we die, love,
   /:So, true love, be well of jealousy.:/

4. "Now I hear the cock are crowing,
   Daylight soon will be drawing near,
   But we will be still for ever
   /:Way down beneath that silent tomb.":/

Come My Brother
or
The Dying Californian

Text and tune: Alice Swain (Glass).

Cf. "The Dying Californian" (Hudson, 1936, p. 221 f.). The tune falls in Bronson's category Ly/I-4 (1946, p. 44), and it is a question whether it is to be described as an hexatonic Lydian mode (as indicated by the key-signature below) or simply as a major lacking the 4th.

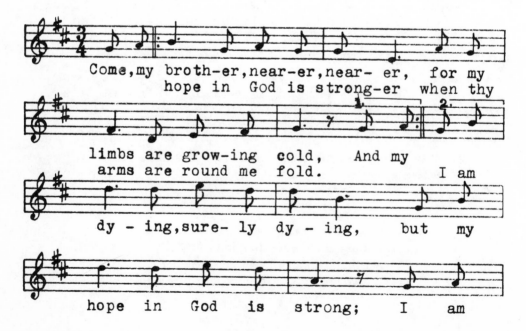

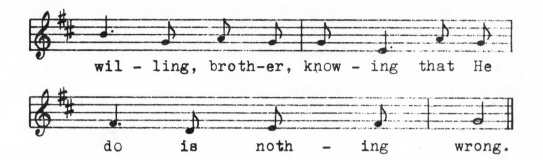

wil - ling, broth-er, know - ing   that   He

do   is   noth - ing   wrong.

1. Come, my brother, nearer, nearer,
   for my limbs are growing cold,
And my hope in God is stronger
   when thy arms are 'round me fold.
I am dying, surely dying,
   but my hope in God is strong;
I am willing, brother, knowing
   that He do is nothing wrong.

2. Tell my father when you meet him,
   I will pray for him in death,
Pray that I may one day meet him
   in a land that's free from sin.
I am dying, surely dying, *etc.*

3. Tell my mother, God resist* her
   now that she is growing old,
Tell, her child would have gladly kissed her
   when his lips grow pale and cold.
I am dying, surely dying,
   but my hope in God is strong;
I am willing, brother, knowing
   that He do is nothing wrong.

* Corruption of 'assist.'

Little Annie Rooney
or
Little Annie Rhoda

Text: Alice Swain (Glass) (in writing).
Tune: Alice Swain (Glass,) Frances Repetto.
Introduced on Tristan by "Shorty" in the *Allen Shaw* (wrecked 1893). Frances
Repetto reported that he jokingly used to sing the last line of the refrain:
                    Little Annie Rooney is my jam tart.
While the older generation referred to the song as "Little Annie Rooney," the
younger ones usually said (and sang) "Little Annie Rhoda" and connected the song
vaguely with Rhoda Ann Cotton, a sister-in-law of Betty Cotton and Martha Green,
who was widowed by the lifeboat accident in 1885 and soon after moved to South
Africa.
        The tune had been adapted to the accordion (see No. 12 in Ditties and Dance
Tunes) and was one of the favorite dance tunes on Tristan.

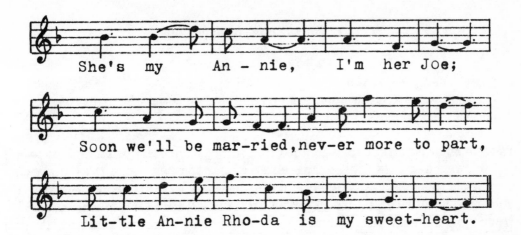

She's my An - nie, I'm her Joe;

Soon we'll be mar-ried, nev-er more to part,

Lit-tle An-nie Rho-da is my sweet-heart.

a) Frances Repetto.

1. Every evening, rain or shine,
   I made a call between eight or nine
   On her who shortly will be mine,
   is little Annie Rhoda.
   She is my sweetheart, I am her beau,
   She is my Annie, I am her Joe;
   Soon we will be married, never more to part,
   Little Annie Rhoda is my sweetheart.

2. We have been engaged close on a year,
   the happy time is drawing near,
   I will wed the one I love so dear,
   is little Annie Rhoda.
   She is my sweetheart, *etc.*

3. The parlour small, but neat and clean,
   and set with taste so seldom seen,
   And you may bet the household queen
   is little Annie Rhoda.
   She is my sweetheart, I am her beau,
   She is my Annie, I am her Joe;
   Soon we will be married, never more to part,
   Little Annie Rhoda is my sweetheart.

Sweet Pretty Polly Perkins from Paddington Green

Text and Tune: John Green.

For a reference to this song by Harry Clifton, see Disher, 1955, p. 164.

1. I'm a poor brokenhearted milkman,
       through grief I give way
   To a young servant girl
       that led me astray;
   She lives in the family
       so neat and so clean,
   She is sweet Pilly-Polly Parkin
       from Padditon Green.
   She was beautiful as a butterfly
       and proud as the Queen,
   She is sweet Pilly-Polly Parkin
       from Padditon Green.

2. Oh, when I ask her to marry me,
   she calls me a muff,
And she said, of your nonsense
   I've had quite enough!
But the same time I told her
   I'd be very kind,
And she said, of your rubbish
   for your better I'll find.
   She was beautiful as a butterfly, *etc.*

3. "Oh, the man that I marry
   must be handsome and bold,
have horses and carriage
   and plenty of gold,
with his hair done in wrinkles
   so curly and long."
And she swore of his whiskets
   must be bushy and strong.
   She was beautiful as a butterfly, *etc.*

4. And a long time after
   this hardhearted girl
She got married to a soldier,
   but he was not a hull,
And he was not a milkman
   but something more worth,
For of ever'n he condunder
   out of two penny worth.
   She was beautiful as a butterfly
   and proud as the Queen,
   She is sweet Pilly-Polly Parkin
   from Padditon Green.

Mary

Text and tune: Arthur Repetto.
Cf. "Mary of the Wild Moor" (Leach, 1955, p. 733f.); Laws, 1957, p. 258;
Mackenzie, 1963, p. 164 f.

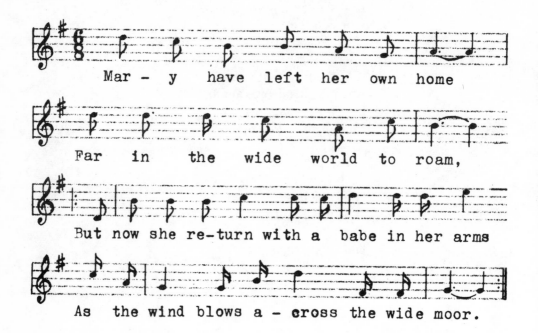

1. Mary have left her own home
   Far in the wide world to roam,
   /:But now she return with a babe in her arms
   As the wind blows across the wide moor.:/

2. "Oh, father, dear father," she cried,
   "Come down and open the door,
   /:For my baby will die with the cold wind and I,
   As the wind blows across the wide moor.":/

3. Her father was deaf to her call,
   He came not to open the door,
   /:So Mary lie dead, but the child still alive,
   Only clasped in his dead mother's arms.:/

4. Next morning her father rise,
 Came down and opened the door,
 /:He found Mary lying dead, but the child still alive,
 Only clasped in his dead mother's arms.:/

William Brown

Text and tune: Arthur Repetto.

1. William Brown was a clever young man,
 First he had leded me from home,
 He led me from my parents, he led me from my home,
 And he left me in this wild world to roam, roam, roam,
 And he left me in this wild world to roam.

2. Six months is past and three more to come;
 One day when poor Willie was rolling by,

"Stop, stop!" cried she, "you'll have a babee
On that same very day you can't deny, ny, ny,
On that same very day you can't deny."

3. "I can deny and I will deny,
You can't tell me where and what time."
"It was in my father's garden beneath that old oak tree
Just when the new town clock was striking nine, nine, nine,
Just when the new town clock was striking nine."

4. He's gone and he's gone to the Lord knows where,
Perhaps he may never will return,
Perhaps he may be lying beneath the mighty deep,
And his body in that salt sea below, low, low,
And his body in that salt sea below.

5. Come all you young and silly young maids,
Come and take a warning unto this;
Never let a young man court you while you's young
Nor a sailor have an inch above your knee, knee, knee,
Nor a sailor have an inch above your knee.

Beer

Text and tune: Henry Green.
　　Henry Green reported having heard this song only once, as sung by sailors on board a visiting British man-of-war. As might be expected, the text is partly corrupt, presumably by the vagueness of Henry's memory. Stanzas 1 and 3, e.g., have been augmented with two extra lines each, which obviously stem from half forgotten stanzas, and which were inserted here by repeating the two first phrases of the tune This corrupt form, however, had already been established as a traditional form in the sense that it was regarded as "correct."
　　The tune stays within the narrow range of a quint, moving between the lower dominant and the second, thus using only five tones of the scale, but without the characteristic gaps of the older pentatonic modes.

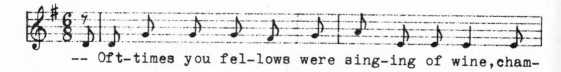
-- Oft-times you fel-lows were sing-ing of wine,cham-

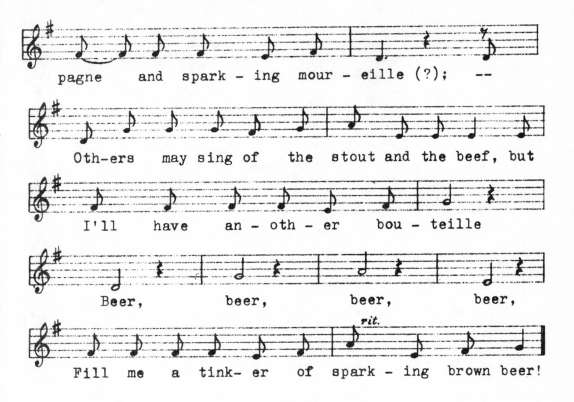

pagne   and   spark - ing   mour - eille (?);   --

Oth-ers   may sing of   the   stout and the beef, but

I'll   have   an - oth - er   bou - teille

Beer,   beer,   beer,   beer,

Fill   me   a   tink- er   of   spark - ing   brown beer!

1. Ofttimes you fellows were singing of wine,
    champagne and sparking moureille (?),
  Others may sing of the stout and the beef,
    but I'll have another bouteille;
  What's good for the rich, what's good for the poor,
    more wholesome and not of so dear,
      Beer, beer, beer, beer,
        Fill me a tinker of sparking brown beer!

2. The seeds of Old England, much better than wine,
    our foes have plenty to fear,
  Our Army and Navy has plenty of beef,
    our Rifle drink glorious brown beer,
      Beer, beer, beer, beer,
        Fill me a tinker of sparking brown beer!

3. You'll see men with red noses and faces high blue
    through rum, gin, brandy, and wine,
  While others are up with the lark in the morning,

so the man to the wall must repair,
Close on the backs and the pound they can spin,
    as when we drink glorious brown beer,
        Beer, beer, beer, beer,
            Fill me a tinker of sparking brown beer!

4. Take away from a man his tobacco and beer,
    if that man should weigh twenty stone,
Just give him a call in two or three weeks,
    you'll find that he's all skin and bone.
        Beer, beer, beer, beer,
            Fill me a tinker of sparking brown beer!

5. Teetotal may spree till he's black in the face,
    you'll see men in everywhere,
The tinker, the taylor, the King and the sailor,
    and likewise a wister may know,
        Beer, beer, beer, beer,
            Fill me a tinker of sparking brown beer!

Ole Dan Tucker

Text and tune: Henry Green.
    This well known blackface minstrel song by Daniel Emmett was brought to
Tristan da Cunha by Thomas (Tom) Glass, who spent fifteen years (1850-1865)
away from Tristan, mostly, it seems, in American whaling ships. Henry Green
learned the song from him. The version published by Paskman and Spaeth (1928, p.
42ff.) has little in common with the Tristan version. For still another version, see
Lomax, 1947, p. 132 f.

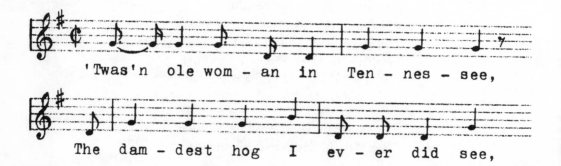

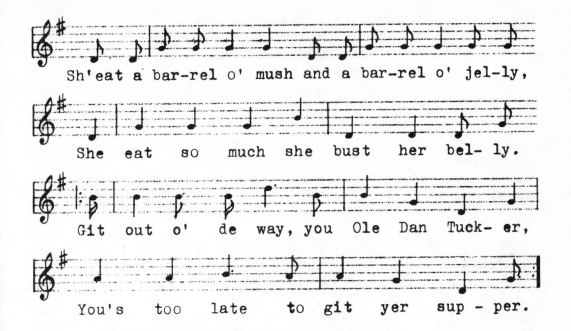

Sh'eat a bar-rel o' mush and a bar-rel o' jel-ly,

She eat so much she bust her bel-ly.

Git out o' de way, you Ole Dan Tuck-er,

You's too late to git yer sup-per.

1. 'Twas'n ole woman in Tennessee,
   The damdest hog I ever did see,
   Sh'eat a barrel o' mush and a barrel o' jelly,
   She eat so much she bust her belly.
   /:Git out o' de way, you Ole Dan Tucker,
   You's too late to git yer supper.:/

2. Ole Dan Tucker and Ole Dan Bull,
   Dey had a race for aste of supper;
   Ole Dan Tucker he beat Dan Bull
   And came to de house and crammed down full.
   Git out o' de way, *etc.*

3. Ole Dan Tucker he came to de town,
   He swallowed a hog's head o' melastes down;
   Hog's head work and melastes bust,
   'Way went Tucker in the thunder dust.
   Git out o' de way, *etc.*

4. Ole Dan Tucker he came to de town,
   And dere he saw some coloured people,

Some was white and some was black,
And some was the colour of chewed tobac.
/:Git out o' de way, you Ole Dan Tucker,
You's too late to git yer supper.:/

Girls from the South

Text and tune: Henry Green.
 This is another blackface minstrel song which Henry Green learned from Tom
Glass, the whaler.

-Mas-ter bought some yel-low girls, he bought 'em from de Souph,

Her hair did curl so ver-y tight she could-n-not shut her mouph.

Yak - yak - ya, yak - yak - ya, girls from de Souph,

Her hair did curl so ver-y tight she could-n-not shut her mouph.

1. Master bought some yellow girls,
   he bought 'em from de Souph,
   Her hair did curl so very tight,
   she could-n-not shut her mouph.
   Yakyakya, yakyakya,
   girls from de Souph,
   Her hair did curl so very tight,
   she could-n-not shut her mouph.

2. Santisoo she took sick,
   dey did-n' know what to do;
   Dey fend her wi' de ole banjo,
   but could-n-not fetch her to.
   Yakyakya, yakyakya, *etc.*

3. Dey took her to de doctor
    to get her mouph so small;
  She drawed one good breaf
    and swallowed de doctor an' all.
  Yakyakya, yakyakya, *etc.*

4. Her eyes dey was so very large,
    dey bo' run into one;
  But when a fly lie on her eye,
    like a June bug in the sun.
  Yakyakya, yakyakya, *etc.*

5. Master had no hooks 'n' nails,
    he had no things like dat,
  But on dat ole darkey's nose
    he hung his coat an' hat.
  Yakyakya, yakyakya,
    girls from de Souph,
  Her hair did curl so very tight,
    she could-n-not shut her mouph.

Happy Darkey
or
Josiphus Orange Blossom

Text and tune: Henry Green.

This blackface minstrel song was brought to Tristan by a sailor in the American sailing ship *Mabel Clark,* which was wrecked at the island in 1878.

Cf. "Josiphus Orange Blossom" (Paskman and Spaeth, 1928, p. 54 ff.).

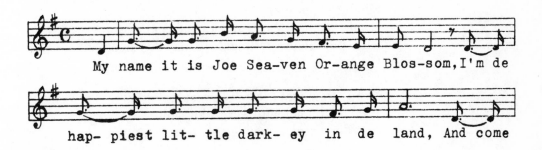

all ye pret-ty girls to play de par-son, I'm a

red - hot hunk - y - dor - y coun - try band.

Red hot, I guess not, I'm de

hap- piest lit- tle dark- ey in de land, And come

all ye pret-ty girls to play de par-son, I'm a

red - hot hunk - y - dor - y coun - try band.

4/3: sline-ly thru' her bed-room win-dow was a-peep-in',I

1. My name it is Joe Seaven Orange Blossom,
   I'm de happiest little darkey in de land,
   And come all ye pretty girls to play de parson,
   I'm a red-hot hunkydory country band.
   Red-hot, I guess not,
   I'm de happiest little darkey in de land,
   And come all ye pretty girls to play de parson,
   I'm a red-hot hunkydory country band.

2. The first time that I saw my sweet Melizzie
   I tried to win her with a great big smile,
   I throw my arm around her waist to kiss her;

"Go 'way," she said, "I do not like your style."
Red-hot, I guess not, *etc.*

3. I thought my Jane Melizzie was a beauty,
   And on her pretty cheeks my eyes could feast,
   And if she had no serious objection,
   Some Sat'day night we patridize the priest.
   Red-hot, I guess not, *etc.*

4. One night when sweetheart on my mind was creepin'
   I thought on my sweetheart I would call,
   So slinely through her bedroom window was a-peepin'
   I saw a sight which did my heart repall.
   Red-hot, I guess not, *etc.*

5. Her teeth and her eye lay on de table,
   And her pretty little curling on de peg,
   And I laugh and shout as long as I was able,
   To see her taking off her wooden leg.
   Oh no, not for Joe,
   I never took Melizzie for a wife,
   For I got straight out o' town, I dusted;
   I never was so sold in all my life.

Over the Water

Text: Henry Green.
Tune: Alice Swain (Glass).
1/1-2, according to Frances Repetto:
          By the Tall Tree River, where I was born,
          Is a hut made of stock of the tall yellow corn.

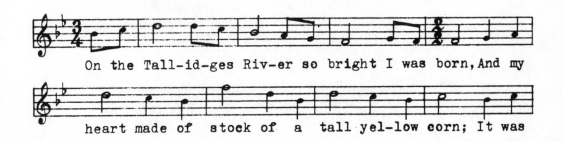

On the Tall-id-ges Riv-er so bright I was born, And my
heart made of stock of a tall yel-low corn; It was

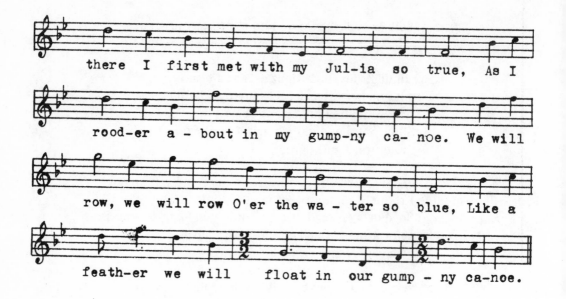

there I first met with my Jul-ia so true, As I rood-er a - bout in my gump-ny ca- noe. We will row, we will row O'er the wa - ter so blue, Like a feath-er we will float in our gump - ny ca-noe.

1. On the Tallidges River so bright I was born,
   And my heart made of stock of a tall yellow corn;
   It was there I first met with my Julia so true,
   As I rooder about in my gumpny canoe.
     We will row, we will row,
     O'er the water so blue,
     Like a feather we will float
     In our gumpny canoe.

2. All day in the fields of sporting a hoe,
   While I think of my Julia and sing as I go,
   While the stars they shine down on my Julia so true,
   As I rooder about in my gumpny canoe.
     We will row, we will row, *etc.*

3. With my hand on the banjo and toil on the oar,
   I will sing of the sea and the rivers which roar;
   We will catch her a bird with the wing of true blue,
   As I rooder about in my gumpny canoe.
     We will row, we will row, *etc.*

4. One night when the streamboat was far, far away,
   We could not get back, so we thought we just stay;

We spied a tall ship with the flag of true blue,
And she took us on tow to our country canoe.
We will row, we will row,
O'er the water so blue,
Like a feather we will float
In our gumpny canoe.

The Spanish Gambaleer

Text: Henry Green.
Tune: Alice Swain (Glass).
    According to Andrew Swain, 3/4-5:
                And if I should be slain,
                You needn't search in vain.

    1. The Spanish gambaleer
      Sat under a tree
      And on his guitar played the tune there;
      The music so sweet
      I ofttimes repeat,
      Songs unto you I will sing, dear.

Say, love, say,
While I'm far away,
Sometimes you may think of me, dear;
Bright sunny days
Will soon fade away,
Believe what I say to be true, dear.

2. I'm off to the war,
   To the war I must go
   To fight for my country and you, dear;
   And if I should fall,
   On you I will call,
   Blessings on you and your country.
     Say, love, say, *etc.*

3. And when the war is o'er,
   Just back I'll return,
   Back to my country and you, dear;
   And if I should be slain,
   You'll surely search in vain,
   For on the battlefield you will find me.
     Say, love, say,
     While I'm far away,
     Sometimes you may think of me, dear;
     Bright sunny days
     Will soon fade away,
     Believe what I say to be true, dear.

Nelly Gray

Text and tune: Alice Swain (Glass).
    The refrain was given a slightly different form by Ben Swain:
        Poor Nelly Gray, they have taken her away,
        I'll never see my darling any more;
        I am sitting by the river and I'm weeping all the day,
        Farewell to the old Kentucky shore.

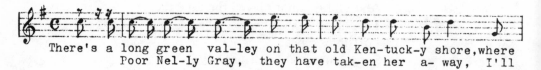
There's a long green val-ley on that old Ken-tuck-y shore, where
       Poor Nel-ly Gray, they have tak-en her a- way, I'll

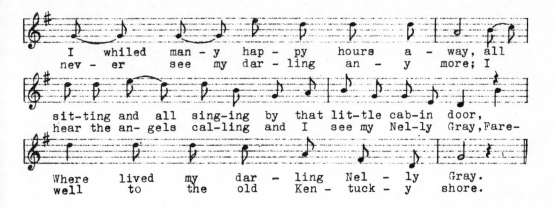

I whiled man - y hap - py hours a - way, all
nev - er see my dar - ling an - y more; I

sit-ting and all sing-ing by that lit-tle cab-in door,
hear the an- gels cal-ling and I see my Nel-ly Gray, Fare-

Where lived my dar - ling Nel - ly Gray.
well to the old Ken - tuck - y shore.

1. There's a long green valley on that old Kentucky shore,
   Where I whiled many happy hours away,
   All sitting and all singing by that little cabin door,
   Where lived my darling Nelly Gray.
      Poor Nelly Gray, they have taken her away,
      I'll never see my darling any more;
      I hear the angels calling and I see my Nelly Gray,
      Farewell to the old Kentucky shore.

2. One night I went to see her, she's gone, the neighbour said,
   The white man has bound her with his chain,
   They have taken her to Georgia for to wear her life away,
   And she toils the cotton and the cane.
      Poor Nelly Gray, they have taken her away, *etc.*

3. My canoe is on the water and my banjo are on tune,
   I'm tired of living any more,
   For my eyes shall look downwards and my song shall be untuned;
   Farewell to the old Kentucky shore.
      Poor Nelly Gray, they have taken her away,
      I'll never see my darling any more;
      I hear the angels calling and I see my Nelly Gray,
      Farewell to the old Kentucky shore.

DITTIES AND DANCE TUNES

No. 1A Chase me, Charlie

Chase me, Charlie!
Chase me, Charlie!
Lost a piece of my drawers!
—— —— —— (?)
and starch 'em on
and send 'em over to me.

No. 1B Step Dance
Alfred Green, accordion.

No. 2. Step Dance
Andrew Swain, fiddle.

No. 3A

Text and tune: Arthur Repetto

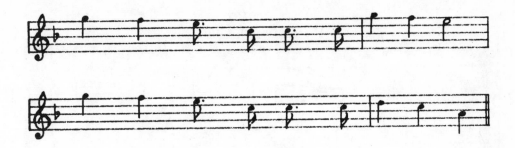

If it weren't any women in the world,
the men they had to do without;
there'd be no more kisses at the garden gate,
no more scratches at the old man's face.

No. 3B. Shottee
Andrew Swain, fiddle.

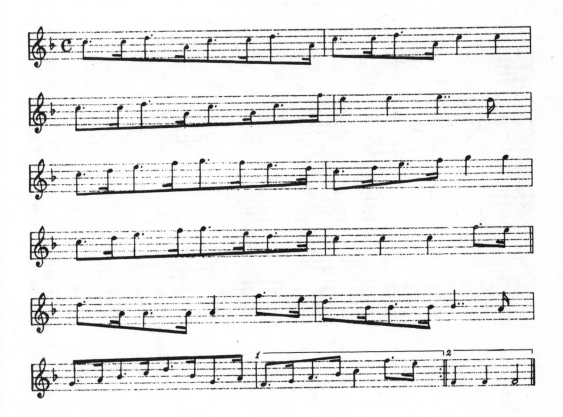

No. 4. Shottee
Andrew Swain, fiddle.

No. 5. Shottee
Andrew Swain, fiddle.

No. 6. Shottee
Alfred Green, accordion.

No. 7. Tapioca's Big Toe (Shottee)
Alfred Green, accordion.

No. 8. Heel - Toe Polka
Alfred Green, accordion

No. 9. Waltz
Alfred Green, accordion.

No. 10. Waltz
Andrew Swain, fiddle.

No. 11. Waltz
Andrew Swain, fiddle.

No. 12. Little Annie Rooney Waltz
Alfred Green, accordion.

No. 13. A Dear Little Maiden
or
After the Ball
Waltz, accordion.

Text: Arthur Repetto (from Frances Repetto).

The tune was accommodated to the words by repeating the first sixteen bars twice, then going on to the last sixteen bars, which were repeated once. Besides, upbeats were added and half notes divided as necessary, in the usual manner.

A dear little maiden sat on her uncle's knee,
Bidding for a story you never hear.
Is, have you a baby? Have you a home?
I have no baby, I have no home,
I had a sweetheart many a year ago,
But now he's gone and left me after the ball.
   After the ball was over,
   After the break of day,
   We were all in the 'all together
   After the ball.
   Many a heart were aching,
   Many a sorrowful tear,
   Many a heart were aching,
   If you could read the mind.

No. 14. All Under the Coconut Tree

Text and tune: Andrew Swain, Arthur Repetto.
   While Andrew Swain had only four verses to this song and inserted the refrain
only after every other verse, Arthur Repetto sang the refrain after each verse and
added verse 5.

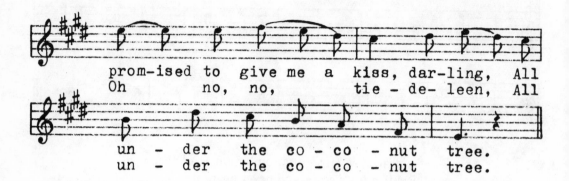

prom-ised to give me a kiss, dar-ling, All
Oh   no, no,   tie - de- leen, All

un - der the co - co - nut tree.
un - der the co - co - nut tree.

1. You promised to give me a kiss, darling,:/ *(thrice)*
   All under the coconut tree.

2. How did you like your kiss, darling?:/ *(thrice)*
   All under the coconut tree.
    Oh no, no, tiedeleen,:/ *(thrice)*
   All under the coconut tree.

3. You promised to marry me, darling,:/ *(thrice)*
   All under the coconut tree.

4. You promised to buy me the ring, darling,:/ *(thrice)*
   All under the coconut tree.
    Oh no, no, tiedeleen,:/ *(thrice)*
   All under the coconut tree.

5. How did you like your chain, darling?:/ *(thrice)*
   All under the coconut tree.
    Oh no, no, tiedeleen,:/ *(thrice)*
   All under the coconut tree.

No. 15. Say Boys
Waltz, accordion.

Text: Arthur Repetto.

Say boys, to every man,
Say boys, work while you can.
Why can't every man
Have three wives?
Ain't that a glorious, curious thing?
Ain't that an angel without any wing?
Say boys, to every man,
Say boys, work while you can.
Why can't every man
Have three wives?

No. 16A

Text and tune: Arthur Repetto.

1. If you want a pretty girl,
    Feed her up with bread and jam,
    Tell her all the lies you can,
    That's the way to git yer girl.
    /:Tarrara-bum-de-ay,
        I got no wife to-day.:/

2. Irish stylish girl is she,
    Brimmen full of 'ciety,
    Not so bad and not so good,
    Just as right as right can be.
    /:Tarrara-bum-de-ay,
        I got no wife to-day.:/

No. 16B. Waltz
Alfred Green, accordion.

No. 17. Waltz
Alfred Green, accordion.

No. 18A

Text and tune commonly known.

I caught a cargie (?) two a day,
two a day, two a day,
I caught a cargie two a day
as walking up the valley way.

No. 18B. Waltz
Alfred Green, accordion.

No. 19. Waltz
Alfred Green, accordion.

No. 20. Waltz
Alfred Green, accordion.

No. 21. Waltz ("stepping part")
Alfred Green, accordion.

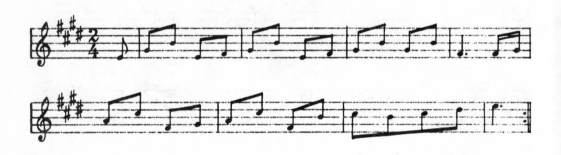

No. 22A. Waltz
Alfred Green (whistling).

This is the way the tune was played by most accordion players, such as Big Charlie Green or George Swain.

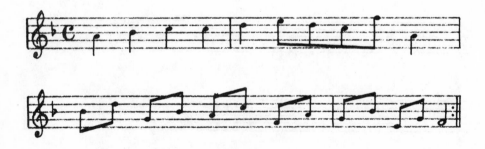

No. *22B. Waltz*
Alfred Green, accordion.

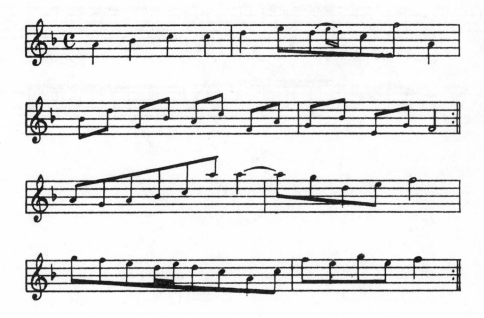

No. 23. Waltz
Alfred Green, accordion.

EPILOGUE

No matter what the particular circumstances may be, every human community, large or small, stands in *some* relationship to a larger cultural system which surrounds it and from which the community receives most of its cultural impulses. When this larger cultural system, the "great tradition" as Redfield calls it,[60] is associated with prestige, authority, or power — as it often is — it takes the form of a "superculture" which may be superimposed upon the community from outside and tends to bring its way of life into conformity with general standards as defined by the superculture, forever chipping away at any peculiarity in custom or outlook.[61] The degree to which any specific community is exposed to these cultural pressures from a surrounding superculture is of course directly dependent upon the amount of contact and the degree to which the community gets involved in the activities of the greater society. Under circumstances of relative isolation, whether natural or artificial, a high degree of cultural autonomy may be retained even by a small community.

From whichever angle one looks at the island community of Tristan da Cunha, the importance of its insular position becomes evident. We have seen how the community was founded and shaped during a period of lively interchange and extensive involvement with sailing ships which in great numbers frequented the waters and shores of the island, and how it was molded into the patterns of the cultural tradition which we have described as the heritage of the seven seas. We have also noted how the almost complete isolation into which the community fell during the latter part of the nineteenth and the first part of the twentieth century left it with a great deal of cultural autonomy, practically untouched by the rapid and extensive cultural changes that took place in the Western world at large during that period. So it was that, in 1938, the Tristan community was still among the rapidly decreasing number of Western communities where traditional songs of an eighteenth and nineteenth century vintage remained a living part of everyday life.

It was a somewhat different Tristan that I returned to in October, 1964, changed in its physical appearance as well as in its way of life. Much was as before. As we were approaching the island from the east, this time in the South African survey ship, the *R. S. A.*, I soon recognized the familiar landmarks: There was Stony Beach, where twenty-seven years ago I had accompanied the Islanders on many a trip for meat or for apples, and where I had heard some of the old songs of Tristan by a blazing bonfire at night. And there was Sandy Point with its shady orchards, Black Sand Beach, and the Rookery. But as we rounded Big Point, where I would have expected to get the first view of the Settlement, there was the first evidence that not all was as before. Where Big Beach and Little Beach had been, a new volcano was reaching its ugly tongue of rugged black lava into the sea, completely concealing from our view the characteristic low profile of Hottentot Point. We had to round another point, as yet unnamed, before we suddenly found ourselves directly off the Settlement, which was now hemmed in to the east by a black wall of lava sloping down from a new cinder cone at the foot of the towering cliffs that form the backdrop of the whole scene as on a stage.

The village looked familiar enough. There were the characteristic stone cottages with their thatched roofs, spread out in picturesque disorder over the grassy slope, almost merging with the landscape as if they had grown out of its very soil, all facing north toward the sun and the sea. But most of them now had concrete walks in front, some of the newer ones had the front wall built of concrete blocks instead of the reddish volcanic soft-stone, and one or two had replaced the traditional thatched roof with the more durable corrugated zink. And wedged between the village and the sea, more prominent to the view, was a straight row of tin-roofed bungalows flanked by two or three even more prominent cement brick buildings that stuck out like sore thumbs in the landscape. This was the "Station," containing the residences of the officials, besides a canteen, a power station and workshops, and a radio station whose tall, white painted masts more than anything else symbolized the fact that the modern era had caught up even with this remote outpost in the South Atlantic.

Since the time of the Norwegian expedition, the situation of the community and its relations to the outside world had changed markedly. It was only a few years after we left the island that the Second World War brought an end to its isolation, perhaps forever. During the war, based on reports that the *Graf Spee* as well as U-boats had been sighted off Tristan, a detachment of the Royal Navy moved in together with South African Air Force personnel and established a camp and a meteorological station. They brought a chaplain and a doctor – the former was not an unfamiliar sight to the Islanders, although they had never seen one in uniform before; but the doctor was the first resident physician on the island. Many of the officers brought their families along, which led to the establishment of a regular school, with a teacher added to the number of "Station people," and with compulsory attendance by the Tristan children as well. With all this came paid labor for the Islanders, and money. A canteen was established which served as a regular country store – and looked like one, too.

After the war, the military establishment on Tristan da Cunha was abandoned. But the island never returned to its former isolation and tranquility. Possibilities and prospects, discovered and discussed by foresighted members of the military establishment, attracted the attention of the outside world. The importance of regular reports from Tristan for weather foreçasts in South Africa had been proven, and the South African Government decided to continue the meteorological station on the island with civilian personnel, which meant continued radio contacts with the outside world and regular visits by supply ships. And an enterprising Navy chaplain, entranced with the unbelievable riches of the fishing grounds around Tristan, aroused the interest of a South African fishing company. The result was the establishment, in 1949, of a permanent fishing industry concerned with the export of frozen rock lobster tails for the American market, with a year-round operation from a land station with a freezing plant, and seasonal operations from two fishing vessels, the *Tristania* and the *Frances Repetto*, with home port in Cape Town. This, of course, meant additional paid labor for the Islanders both in the "factory," which employed only Islanders, and on board the fishing vessels, where Islanders were hired along with African and colored fishermen from the Cape. It also meant the continuation of a colony of salaried outsiders and their families, with all that this entailed in terms of monetary exchange for goods and services, the maintenance of a school, a fairly well stocked canteen, and even a public bar and a movie house with weekly shows, all run by the company. Finally, it gave rise to regular connections, by ship and by radio, with Cape Town and the world at large. On the whole, the establishment of a permanent industry, however modest, pulled the Tristan community back into the commerce of the civilized world and appeared to bring an end to the subsistence economy that had developed during the long period of isolation.

Furthermore, with all this going on, the Colonial Office in London found it necessary to establish a formal administration on Tristan da Cunha. So far, the community had managed fairly well for some 130 years without such administration, and as far as the Islanders were concerned, they would probably have preferred to keep it that way. The principle of equality, which founded their community in the first place, is still very much with them, and four generations of insular freedom from any form of governmental control has turned them into rugged individualists. Besides, they saw no need for an administration in a community where there were no laws, no crime (at least none worth mentioning), and where every potential dispute is settled before it starts by time-honored conventions.

But the officials in the Colonial Office did not see it that way. To their bureaucratic minds, the orderly anarchy of Tristan da Cunha had always been a vexing anomaly, and with the presence of a "colony" of "expatriates" (as the colonial jargon goes), it was impossible to keep it up any longer. At first, magisterial powers were delegated to the resident doctor or priest. But in January 1950, the first appointed administrator landed on Tristan, with his family following shortly after. The Colonial Office also took on the responsibility for keeping a medical officer and a nurse, a teacher, and an agricultural officer on the island. To engage the Islanders in this formal administration — in ostensible "democratic" fashion an Island Council was set up, with proper "committees" and other governmental and legislative institutions, in which the Islanders obediently participated by appointment, later even by general elections, but always, of course, under proper supervision.

However, an even closer and more intimate contact with modern civilization was in store for the Tristan Islanders. In October 1961, for the first time in the history of the community, the long restive volcano of Tristan da Cunha stirred into an eruption which destroyed the factory and threatened to engulf the settlement itself. The island was evacuated, and the entire population of 264 men, women, and children were taken to England, where they eventually were resettled at Calshot, near Southampton, in a semi-industrial area that seemed to offer a variety of job opportunities. As far as the Colonial Office was concerned, it was obviously intended as a permanent evacuation of Tristan da Cunha, and the plan was apparently to give the Islanders a good start and then leave them alone. The British Government provided them with good housing in a settlement designed for Royal Air Force personnel, and all who were able got jobs — in garages and service stations, in road construction and maintenance, in a nearby oil refinery, or in various kinds of factories.

The Tristan Islanders, on the other hand, assumed all the time as a matter of course, that their stay in England was only temporary. Two young Islanders who had returned to Tristan as guides for a scientific expedition, came back to Calshot with favorable reports: the eruption had subsided, the village had been spared, and the cattle were grazing peacefully on the grassy slopes beside the new volcano. But not a word was received from the authorities. With their deeply ingrained respect for the superculture of the British Commonwealth and with their indelible faith in the benevolence of Her Majesty's Government, it took some time for the Islanders to realize what was happening to them and that the Government had no intention at all of making arrangements for their return to Tristan. In this desperate situation, completely lost in the intricate channels and pitfalls of a bureaucratic machinery, the Islanders pleaded for help wherever they thought they could get it and finally decided to go home on their own.

Confronted with such determination on the part of the Islanders, the Colonial Office reversed its policy and promised to take care of all arrangements for a return to the island. However, it took almost an additional year and a half before the promise was carried out. Finally, in November 1963, the community returned to Tristan da Cunha after a "brush with civilization" that had lasted for more than two years.

All these events could not fail to have an impact upon the Tristan community and its whole style of life. A visit to Calshot during the summer of 1962 revealed, for one thing, a definitely more cosmopolitan outlook. And a six months' stay among the Islanders during 1964 and 1965, one year after their return to Tristan, confirmed the impression. These islanders are not any more the conservative. tradition-directed lot that we knew in 1938.

It is obvious at first glance that the cash economy provided by the fishing industry has made a great difference in the lives of the Tristan Islanders. A higher level of living was quite evident, not only from the cemented walks in front of their houses but also in the interior decoration and furnishings as well as in the quality of their homemade canvas longboats. Obviously, there was no longer a shortage of woodwork and paint, nails and tools. Already "before the volcano" — which has become an important epoch on Tristan da Cunha — technical improvements had been introduced, partly at the expense of the company or the administration, such as modern water supply and sanitation. And the permanent presence of a prestigeful group of outsiders as well as a canteen primarily stocked to the needs of that group had gone a long way in breaking down the old conservatism of the Islanders and their time-honored customs in dress and food habits. With it, of course, came also tooth decay and other civilized ailments.

When the Islanders arrived in England, they were eager to point out and demonstrate that they were not as old-fashioned and backward as people seemed to think. Although they had to learn a lot of things from scratch, from catching the right bus to dialing a telephone or ringing a doorbell, they rapidly acquired familiarity with modern means of transportation and communication. Many of the younger men procured such important prestige symbols as motorcycles or scooters, and bicycles were quite common among the teenage boys. The younger women in particular quickly abandoned the heavy stockings of homespun wool and the still somewhat lengthy skirts and adopted a more modern style of dress, although some of their elders frowned at the indecency of short skirts, nylons, and low necks. Lipstick and nail polish became fairly common, and more and more women had their hair cut and even learned the use of the beauty parlor. In their homes, they soon got used to electric cooking, radio, and television, and after some initial confusion they even learned to buy on the installment plan. On the whole, an amazingly quick adaptation to the patterns and symbols of modern civilization was apparent.

Finally, when the Tristan Islanders returned home, they did not abandon the new attitudes, tastes, and habits that they had acquired in England, and they brought with them a lot of the twentieth-century technology to add to what they had before. M/S *Bornholm*, the Danish ship chartered by the Colonial Office to bring the Islanders back to Tristan, did indeed carry a most "general cargo" on that voyage, and as landing operations proceeded, with the Tristan longboats ferrying back and forth between the ship and the rugged shore, the whole length of the beach was strewn with a motley of goods, as if the whole community were returning from a gigantic shopping trip. There were all kinds of trunks and boxes, bags and bundles, chairs and tables and other furniture, bedding, kerosene cooking stoves and refrigerators, rugs for the floors, record players and bathtubs, transistor radios, and even tape recorders. And for each record player one could be sure that somewhere, carefully wrapped in polythene, there would be a stack of records of the latest pop music.

Nevertheless, a closer acquaintance with the "new" Tristan soon revealed that these changes, however conspicuous, did not penetrate very far below the surface of the Islanders' social life. From an economic point of view, it should be noted that the cash trading provided by the fishing industry, although it meant a considerable rise in the Islanders' level of living, did not supplant the traditional subsistence economy of the community. The backbone of the Tristan existence is still the potato crop, the sheep, and the cattle raised by each family for its own consumption. All that the fishing industry provided was a cash supplement to an overwhelmingly predominant subsistence economy. And two years of complete submergence in a total cash economy based on tough competition for jobs and profits was apparently not enough even to put a dent in the social structure of the community with its ethical principles of mutual aid and voluntary cooperation along well-established kinship lines.

So it did not take long for the Tristan Islanders after their return to fall back into the complex but familiar patterns of reciprocity, where every major task became a social event of great significance, whether it was building a house or thatching a roof, going to Stony Beach for meat or sailing to Nightingale for birds' fat or eggs.

————————————————

It was in this atmosphere, where work and play were inseparably intermingled, that the old songs had thrived so well. Yet it was not entirely unexpected to find that today the old song tradition of Tristan da Cunha is practically dead. There are of course still people around who remember some of the old songs, and a song collector may still be able to bring them out — for a price. But for the most part, traditional songs of an eighteenth or even nineteenth century vintage are not any more a living part of the cultural tradition of Tristan da Cunha. They are not any more in actual use and are regarded and treated as peculiar relics of a bygone day.

One must assume that the development took place gradually. Reliable reports from Tristan are rare even during this period of traffic and commerce. But the changing attitude of the Tristan Islanders to the old song tradition is well illustrated by two accounts from persons who visited the island at different times between 1940 and 1960.

D. M. Booy was one of a group of naval telegraphists manning the signal station established on Tristan during World War II. In January 1943 he joined a party of some thirty-five Islanders going in six longboats to fetch guano from Inaccessible. In his very descriptive, almost poetic language he gives this account of an evening on the shores of this uninhabited island:

. . .When the guano-collecting was finished, all the men assembled round a fire
that had been lit close under the cliff-face. We sat in a tight circle gazing intently at
the flames, our backs turned on the sea, as if to shut out the wild sighing of the surge
and the keening of its birds. The cry of the petrel was particularly disturbing, a sharp
sobbing wail that sounded intolerably like that of a child in distress.

To repel the sense of desolation with which the island was trying to detroy us, a
sing-song was proposed, but the natural diffidence of the islanders interposed an
obstacle. Many of them had good bass voices but at first no one was willing to sing a
solo. Attempts were made to persuade George Glass, or 'Gillie' as he was called, but
he would only reiterate in an embarrassed rumble: 'Oi doan' know no sawngs!' or 'Oi
ain't got no wice!' At last, without preliminary, Arthur Repetto burst into the
opening verse of a long ballad about the ship *Golden Wanitee*. He was singing in a
high, strained voice, far above his normal deep speaking tones. With every chorus the
rest of the men would join in:
> 'An' they sink 'im in the lowlands,
> Lowlands lowlands,
> An' they sink 'im in the lowlands low.'

This song went on for a long time and was hardly less doleful than the sobbing
of the petrels. Afterwards old Henry Green proffered a quavering solo, then Dick
Swain sang a rollicking but unintelligible song about a certain 'Whisky Wan.' [62]

Twelve years later, in October 1955, a British scientific expedition to Gough
Island spent some time on Tristan surveying the plant and bird life of the island and
making films and tape recordings of the community. Martin Holdgate who
succeeded to the position of leadership of the expedition after two predecessors had
been disabled, describes the activities:

. . .A meeting of the Island Council was filmed and recorded, as were many other
aspects of local life. On two evenings some of the older men came and sang songs that
have been handed down on the island from the early days of the Settlement. They are
a strange mixture, these songs. There are some which speak of the War of American
Independence, and of times when
> . . .the blood runs streaming,
> Streams and streams at Bunker's Hill,
and when 'the sons of Freedom' are exhorted to remember 'the lives that were lost in
Americay'. Yet other songs are as emphatically English, speaking of Easter Day on
Westminster Bridge, or our old friend 'pretty Polly Perkins of Paddington Green'.
Georgie Swain flung himself into these songs with great vigour, and was ably
supported by his companions.[63]

In the first instance we have songs performed in a natural situation as a living
part of the Islanders' social life; in the second, the songs have been put on exhibit,
strictly for the benefit of curious outsiders.

When I visited the Tristan Islanders in Calshot during the summer of 1962, there were no songs on their lips. The situation was not conducive to it. The Colonial Office wanted the Islanders to stay in England and had closed its files on Tristan da Cunha. The Islanders wanted to go home but found that their repeated applications and petitions to the Colonial Office, which was the only government agency they knew, remained unanswered. In spite of their rapid and willing adjustment to the working and living conditions of their new environment, they were frustrated, depressed, and desperate. In this atmosphere there was not much activity in terms of social gatherings and entertainment. In the evenings the Islanders would mostly sit in their houses, and the former Royal Air Force settlement, where the Government had put them up, was as dead as a graveyard.

Even their weddings, of which there were several during their stay in England, were subdued and austere, stripped of most of the social trimmings that used to accompany such occasions. Some of them would include a reception and a dance but mostly arranged by helpful outsiders, and the Islanders would for the most part just go through the motions in a passive sort of way — in the same manner as with anything arranged for them by well-meaning members of the prestigeful superculture.

The well-known folklorist and song collector, Maud Karpeles, went to Calshot and obtained a couple of songs on tape from a reluctant Mary Swain. She also witnessed some of the old dances and recorded the music.[64] But again, this was an exhibit performance for the benefit of an outsider.

As soon as final decisions had been made about the return of the Islanders to Tristan da Cunha, the community came back to life. Several of the Islanders bought themselves new accordions, record players, transistor radios, tape recorders, and guitars to take home to Tristan. Of course, the record players, radios, and tape recorders as well as the guitars were a clear indication that the entertainment patterns had changed. However, as the main party of Islanders were returning to Tristan on board the *Bornholm,* there appears to have been a lively but, as it turned out, shortlived revival of the older pattern. A dance or two were arranged on board, at which Charlie Green played the accordion, presenting a number of tunes of an unmistakable late nineteenth century vintage, including one introduced to Tristan by "Shorty," a castaway from the sailing ship *Allen Shaw,* wrecked at the island in 1893.[65] And on one or two occasions, Arthur Repetto, now at the age of 63, entertained with a couple of songs of the old tradition: "Over the Water" and "The Golden Vanity."[66]

During my recent six months' stay on Tristan, through the southern summer of 1964/65, it was quite evident that the patterns of entertainment had changed. The basic forms of social life were still the same as before, with a few additions. The old school house behind the church had been torn down long ago. In its place, a much larger and more stately building had been erected, with a large dancing hall which on Wednesday nights served as a movie theater, and a smaller "pub" which on rarer

Fred Swain in 1962

Mary Swain in 1962

occasions (whenever the Administrator felt like it) served as the meeting room of the Island Council but otherwise was used as intended: a place where men and youths could gather in the evening for a game of pool or cards or dart and a drink for sixpence a tot; but there were no songs.

The new dancing hall was used quite as frequently as the old one had been, and the occasions were the same as before: Boxing Day, New Year's, Queen's Day, Easter, besides weddings and big birthdays. The officers of the fishing vessels usually gave a farewell dance before leaving at the end of the season.

The general pattern of these dances was unchanged. The women would sit on benches along one wall, sometimes on each other's laps in two or three layers, while the men would be standing around the floor or moving, more or less obviously, in the direction of their chosen partners for the next dance. The benches along the other wall would be occupied by onlookers, older women with their knittings or with sleeping grandchildren in their arms, and men with no intention of taking part in the keen competition for dancing partners. As the music started for another tune, each man would grab his partner by the wrist and gently drag her onto the floor — only to see her disappear like a flash back to the sideline as soon as the tune was finished. But young courting couples would see their way to disappear quietly (if not unnoticed) for a bit of fresh air in the coolness of the dark night.

There was one big difference from 1938. The music was modern dance music, often of South African origin and style, played on a record player, and the dances were a shuffling "fox trot," jitterbug or "jive," and an occasional twist. There would only be a short interlude of accordion music in the old style with the corresponding dances: waltz, step dance, and shottee. During the inevitable intermission, the refreshments — now mostly consisting of canned orange juice and biscuits from the Island Store — were accompanied not by song but by soft music from the record player.

Even the New Year's Eve mummers were without any songs. The custom is still very much alive. Men, both old and young, would go about the preparations with great vigor. For weeks they would be working in deepest secret on their disguising "outfits," including grotesque masks made out of rags and bits of sheepskin or cowskin, sometimes with bullock's horns or other attributes. On New Year's Eve they would gather at the Administrator's house, which now, with the increased number of people, is the only house on the island apart from the Village Hall which can accommodate them all at one time. Then, instead of moving through the village in one group as the custom used to be, they would break up into smaller groups of five or six or less and go from house to house. An occasional accordion or mouth organ could be heard as the mummers moved around the village. In each house, as before, the women would wait for their boisterous guests with tea and biscuits; there would be the usual pantomime, each mummer acting out his part of mock threat and intimidation; and there would be the usual guessing game, the women trying to unmask the mummer by pronouncing his name. But only in the Administrator's house was there a song — again, at the Administrator's pressing request, Arthur

Repetto presented "The Golden Vanity" in his usual high pitch, straining his natural bass voice to the limit. This was the only time during my recent visit to Tristan that a solo in the old style was performed in anything resembling a natural situation.

Most of the old singers, whose songs I had written down on my first visit to the island, had passed on. An influenza epidemic in 1948 took old Henry Green and his sister, Frances Repetto, as well as old Ben Swain. Ben's older brother Andrew Swain, the fiddler, had died the previous year. Old Sam Swain survived the flu epidemic but died the following year at the ripe old age of 92. His daughter Lily Green died in another influenza attack in 1951. She was survived ten years by her husband Alfred Green, the accordion player, but in 1961, shortly after arrival in England, he and his brother John fell victims to the respiratory diseases of the modern world.

Fred Swain, now the oldest man on the island, is still around, and so is his wife, Mary, as full of vitality as ever. And many others remain who used to entertain with songs, such as Fred's brothers James, George, and Dick. But they do not sing anymore, at least not in public — not because they have grown old, rather because their songs have grown old to the changing taste of their audience.

Arthur Repetto seemed to be the only one available and willing to sing one of the old songs to a large audience, and his performance was mostly limited to the one favorite song, "The Golden Vanity." He was the one who boasted in 1938 that he knew "hundreds of songs." If he did, he had certainly forgotten most of them — through lack of use, as he explained to me himself. He once gave me a song session for my tape recorder; but his repertoire was soon exhausted. It included a couple of songs of more recent origin, such as "Red Sails in the Sunset," and the rollicking "Whisky Wan" that Booy had heard Dick Swain perform during a trip to Inaccessible in 1943 — it was quite as unintelligible this time. Of the old time songs I got only three: "A Poor Anxious Woman," "William Brown," and of course "The Lowlands," which was the title that Arthur usually gave to "The Golden Vanity."

That there should be some variations in the songs over a period of twenty-seven years is only to be expected. Even one and the same singer may have developed new habits or mannerisms in his performance as shown by the version of "The Rich Merchant" obtained from Mary Swain in 1962 by Maud Karpeles as compared with the version that I took up from the same singer in 1938.[67] On the other hand, Arthur Repetto remembered "William Brown" quite well, and although he was a little reluctant at first to sing it to the tape because, as he said, "it's a little rough," his performance of it varied in no significant way from the version he had given me in 1938.

Especially when a song is transmitted from one person to another, some changes or omissions are almost bound to occur, either by "creative forgetting" or just plain forgetting. An example of such reduction, with some rearrangement, is the version of "Over the Water" presented by Arthur Repetto on board the *Bornholm* on the way back to Tristan. This used to be Henry Green's song, and it was from

Arthur Repetto
in 1965

Fred and Mary Swain
in their home on Tristan in 1965.
The door in the background was salvaged
from the wreck of the American bark *Mabel Clark*
in 1878

him that Arthur had picked up most of his songs, apparently including this one. The tune is unchanged (see p. 111):

Over the Water

Text: Arthur Repetto, 1963

    1. . . . . . . .so bright where I was born, [68]
      Was a heart made of stoke of that tall yellow corn.
      It was there I first met with my Yulia so true,
      As I roder about in our comp'ny canoe.
        We will row, we will row
        O'er the water so blue,
        Like a feather we will float
        In our comp'ny canoe.

    2. With my hand on the banjo and toil to the oar
      I will sing to the seas and the rivers which roar,
      While the stars they shine down on my Yulia so true
      As I roder about in our comp'ny canoe.
        We will row, we will row, *etc.*

    3. One night when the steamboat was far, far away,
      And we could not got back, so we thought we jus' stay,
      And we spied a tall ship with the flag of true blue,
      And she took us in tow to our comp'ny canoe.
        We will row, we will row
        O'er the water so blue,
        Like a feather we will float
        In our comp'ny canoe.

In some cases, the variations from 1938 to 1965 are of such a nature that they can only be explained by assuming different lines of transmission. Such is certainly the case with Arthur Repetto's version of "A Poor Anxious Woman" as compared with the version I obtained from Fred Swain in 1938 (p. 61). Again, Arthur had picked up the song from his uncle, Henry Green, who generally represented the Green line of transmission, while Fred probably had his version from the Swain line. In this case, the version obtained in 1965 seems to be better preserved in some respects, although it is obviously not complete:

A Poor Anxious Woman

Text and tune: Arthur Repetto, 1965

A poor anx-ious wom-an sat watch-ing one day, Her

hus-band, the sai- lor at sea.   She

sat by the win- dow with tears in her eyes   To

lis-ten at the mourn-   ful tale   Oh, he's

on- ly gone home with   a friend,   Oh, he's

on- ly gone home with   a friend,   And he

tell me   to tell   you he'll meet you a-gain,For he's

on- ly gone home with   a friend.

1. A poor anxious woman sat watching one day,
   Her husband, the sailor at sea.
   She sat by the window with tears in her eyes
   To listen at the mournful tale:
       Oh, he's only gone home with a friend,
       Oh, he's only gone home with a friend,
       And he tell me to tell you he'll meet you again,
       For he's only gone home with a friend.

2. I can't understand you, the woman reply,
   Why Jack has not come home today,
   For as soon as the ship in the harbour arrive,
   I never yet know him to stay.
       Oh, he's only gone home with a friend, *etc.*

3. So make your mind easy, the sailor reply,
   He's free from all trouble and fear.
   Your Jackie is dead, and he's not gone long,
   He's gone with the angels to dwell,
   And he tell me to tell you he'll meet you again,
   For he's only gone home with a friend.
       Oh, he's only gone home with a friend,
       Oh, he's only gone home with a friend,
       And he tell me to tell you he'll meet you again,
       For he's only gone home with a friend.

Old William Rogers, commonly known as Blind William, was bedridden during the return trip to Tristan. He died in October 1963, just one month after the resettlement. In his cabin on board the *Bornholm,* in a small but remarkably clear voice, he sang a few songs for Roland Svensson. Among them was "All Under the Coconut Tree," which I had obtained in 1938 from Andrew Swain and from Arthur Repetto (p.125f). Blind William did not reveal from whom he had learned the song, but again it is obvious, particularly from the variations in the tune, that he had it from a different source, presumably a different line of transmission on the island. One characteristic of Blind William's version is that he opened the song with the chorus:

All Under the Coconut Tree

Text and tune: William Rogers, 1963

Oh, no, no, dy, darlin', :/ *(thrice)*
All under the coconut tree.

1. How do you like your chain, darlin'? :/ *(thrice)*
   All under the coconut tree.
   Oh, no, no, dy, darlin', :/ *(thrice)*
   All under the coconut tree.

2. You promised to buy me a ring, darlin', :/ *(thrice)*
   All under the coconut tree.
     Oh, no, no, dy, darlin', :/ *(thrice)*
     All under the coconut tree.

3. You promised that you would marry me, :/ *(thrice)*
   All under the coconut tree.
     Oh, no, no, dy, darlin', :/ *(thrice)*
     All under the coconut tree.

A slight difference between the Green and Swain lines of transmission may be seen again in the case of "The Golden Vanity." In 1938, this song was usually presented by Old Sam Swain (p.75). It was considered his song to the extent that I never heard anyone else perform it. Apparently, Henry Green knew the song in a slightly different version, and it was this version that Arthur Repetto picked up and made his favorite number. Presumably after Old Sam Swain had passed away, it became Arthur's song.[69]

The Lowlands
or
The Golden Vanity

Text and tune: Arthur Repetto, 1965

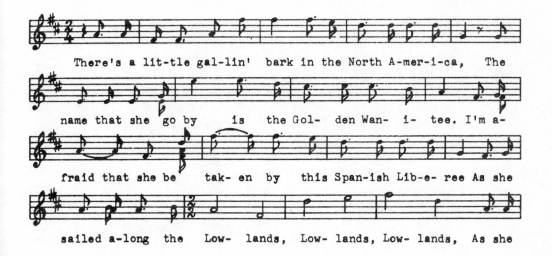

There's a lit-tle gal-lin' bark in the North A-mer-i-ca, The name that she go by is the Gol- den Wan- i- tee. I'm a-fraid that she be tak- en by this Span-ish Lib-e- ree As she sailed a-long the Low- lands, Low- lands, Low- lands, As she

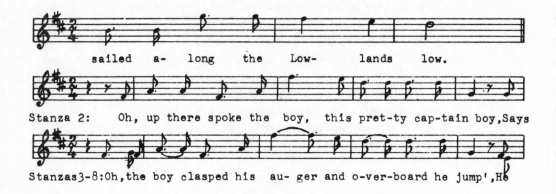

sailed   a-   long   the   Low-   lands   low.

Stanza 2:   Oh, up there spoke the   boy,   this pret-ty cap-tain boy,Says

Stanzas3-8:Oh,the boy clasped his   au- ger and o-ver-board he jump',He

1. There's a little gallin' bark in the North America,
   The name that she go by is *The Golden Wanitee.*
   I'm afraid that she be taken by this Spanish Liberee
   As she sailed along the Lowlands, Lowlands, Lowlands,
   As she sailed along the Lowlands low.

2. Oh, up there spoke the boy, this pretty captain boy,
   Says, Captain, what you give to me if the wessel I destroy?
   Oh, I'll give you gold and silver, my daughter for your bride
   If you sink her in the Lowlands, Lowlands, Lowlands,
   If you sink her in the Lowlands low.

3. Oh, the boy clasped his auger and overboard he jump',
   He swammed and he swam to the Spanish Liberee,
   Oh, he swammed and he swam to the Spanish Liberee,
   But he was sinking in the Lowlands, Lowlands, Lowlands,
   But he was sinking in the Lowlands low.

4. Oh, two holes he borded once, two holes he borded twice,
   While some were playing cards and the others were shaking dice,
   Oh, while some were playing cards and the water were floating in,
   But he sunk her in the Lowlands, Lowlands, Lowlands,
   But he sunk her in the Lowlands low.

5. Oh, he swammed and he swam to his own ship again,
   Cried, Captain, pick me up for I'm sinking in the sea,
   Oh, cried, Captain, pick me up for I'm sinking in the sea,
   And I'm sinking in the Lowlands, Lowlands, Lowlands,
   And I'm sinking in the Lowlands low.

6. Pick you up, says the Captain, is a thing I'll never do,
   I'll shoot you, I'll drown you, I'll do it with good will,
   Oh, I shan't give you gold nor my daughter for your bride,
   But I'll sink you in the Lowlands, Lowlands, Lowlands,
   But I'll sink you in the Lowlands low.

7. Oh, he swammed and he swam to the other side again,
   And there 'e saw'r'is shipmate, and bitter he did cry.
   Oh, cried, shipmate, pick me up for I'm sinking in the sea,
   And I'm sinking in the Lowlands, Lowlands, Lowlands,
   And I'm sinking in the Lowlands low.

8. Oh, his shipmate picked 'im up, and on the deck he die,
   They rolled 'im up in a hammick and lower'im over the side,
   Oh, they rolled 'im up in a hammick and lowered 'im over the side
   And he was burried in the Lowlands, Lowlands, Lowlands,
   And he was burried in the Lowlands low.

This was in fact the only song of the old tradition which had survived the transition to a new style and taste. According to Captain Scott, Master of the *Tristania,* a version of "The Golden Vanity" was occasionally heard among the young Tristan Islanders who worked as fishermen on board his ship, although they did not seem to know the song too well. They used to sing it in unison, and the story was somewhat distorted in a garbled mix-up of the stanzas.[70] It is worth noting that to the younger Islanders this garbled version had become the established form to the extent that any deviation from it was regarded as a "mistake." This was illustrated by an interesting episode during a cookout in front of the Doctor's house in January 1965.

The fishing ships had just returned from their Christmas holiday to start the "small season." Present at the cookout were a few Station people and two or three officers of the *Tristania* when Captain Scott appeared with a young Tristan couple and joined the party. In the somewhat strained atmosphere that always resulted when there was a mixture of Islanders and Station people, the young Islander, who was one of Captain Scott's favorite fishermen, suggested a sing-song. Eventually, in proper Tristan fashion, I allowed myself to be persuaded into singing "The Golden Vanity" as I had heard Old Sam Swain sing it twenty-seven years ago, feeling fairly safe with such authority behind me. However, the young Islander proceeded, rather rudely in fact, to interrupt me with corrections, and when I again invoked the authority of Old Sam Swain, he declared that "there was a lot of mistakes" in the way the old-timers sang the song.

It is probably true that style and taste are among the most vulnerable parts of any culture and therefore most readily subject to change. We have already noted that this may be an important factor in the transmission of cultural tradition, particularly under conditions of extensive intercultural contacts. Especially in the field of entertainment, as in other forms of art expression, there seems to be in every culture a search for new forms that are exciting, if only because they are new. And when new alternative forms of expression are offered by a prestigeful superculture, particularly when they come through such technical marvels as the record player or the radio and are presented by world-known performers, there is, as we know, hardly any resistance.

Besides, it may well be that the old song tradition of Tristan da Cunha had grown stale. We have seen that some of the songs current on Tristan in 1938 were already in an advanced stage of corruption and distortion due to the usual hazards of oral transmission, while others were infected with unintelligible lines and phrases which were supported by a purely phonetic memory and made little or no sense in the context. Also, the combined repertoire of the community was rather limited, with little or no chance of renewal in a style that would be compatible with the old.

Finally, the performance of the old songs was sometimes of a quality that even the Tristan Islanders found lacking. This is especially important in a tradition where a song is closely associated with a particular performer, and it may result in the complete elimination of the song from living tradition since it would be improper for any one else to pick it up to improve the performance. I suspect that for many of the songs current on Tristan in 1938 their survival was partly due to the fact that there were no available alternatives, and it would probably take less than a Frank Sinatra and the prestige of a phonograph to replace them.

Record players had been present on the island for some time. In the 1920s, King George V had presented the community with a phonograph of the old wind-up type together with a collection of records with popular tunes, mostly dance music. Occasionally, the Islanders would also hear phonograph music on board passing ships. This is probably how they adopted a few tunes of more recent origin, such as the ditty, "If you want a pretty girl," which was a favorite in the Western world during the time of World War I, or Weatherly's popular "Danny Boy," which Alice Swain had picked up from a record in her father's possession. But as long as there was only one record player on the island, there was no threat to the old song tradition.

It must be assumed that the military establishments during World War II brought new musical impulses to Tristan. This is when the isolation and cultural autonomy of the island started to break down. However, although a militia of Islanders was indeed organized, it appears that the involvement of the Islanders in the affairs of the outsiders was quite limited, and the social distance to the representatives of the prestigeful superculture, be they officers or enlisted men, was still pronounced.

It was the South African fishing vessels, more than anything else, that finally broke down the cultural isolation of Tristan da Cunha. These fishing vessels were manned by "European," i. e., White officers who were themselves fishermen and seamen by trade and had a professional appreciation of the Islanders' incredible skill as boatmen, and by African and Cape Colored seamen and fishermen whom the Islanders soon discovered as being considered inferior to themselves, not only in skills but also in social status. And the fishing industry was an affair in which the Islanders got actively involved as a number of them were hired as fishermen and deck hands on board the ships.

Not since the days of the sailing ships had the Islanders been in such close physical and social contact with outsiders. The social status they occupied on board, somewhere between the officers and the crew, is interesting and significant. No secret was made of their privileged status. They had separate quarters, somewhat better than those of the African and Cape Colored fishermen, and in their spare time, they apparently felt quite confident to associate rather freely with the officers — more so in the *Frances Repetto* than in the *Tristania*. On the other hand, in their work they were closely associated with the Blacks and, as the Islanders' racial prejudices are not pronounced, they would occasionally participate in the spare time social gatherings of the fishermen, too.

And the Africans had music, live music, with song, mouth organ, and guitar. It was mostly modern pop music, picked up from phonograph records of predominantly American make and origin, but with a definite touch of the South African with its conglomerated tradition of Boer, Zulu, and Xhosa influences.

It was this music, supplemented by phonograph records, that offered the alternative necessary to replace the old song tradition on Tristan. Two brothers, Basil and Ches Lavarello, with no particular connection with any of the main transmission lines of the old song tradition, appear to have pioneered in transferring this kind of singing from the fishing vessels to the community itself. They got themselves shiny guitars, ordered by mail from Cape Town, and Ches (short for Cheseldon) learned from a Zulu on the *Tristania* how to handle a mouth organ and a guitar simultaneously. Soon the Tristan houses would resound with such songs as *Suikerbossie* — always sung in Afrikaans although none of the Islanders knew the language — and *Zambisi*, but also such American favorites as *Red River Valley, Falling in Love,* and many others. An occasional kwela (a Zulu dance tune) was also in the repertoire. Some of the songs were adapted to local conditions — such as "She'll be wearing Tristan stockings when she comes," the newly introduced nylons notwithstanding — and very popular was a song, to the tune of "Galway Bay," about "a little ship called the *Frances Repetto*" (or the *Tristania,* as the case may be) which boldly "sails far across the mighty ocean, fifteen hundred miles from Table Bay."

These songs were not performed as self-conscious solos to an attentive audience but as unison group singing where everybody joined in who cared to lift his voice. And they belonged particularly in groups of young people, in the relaxed, informal, and unceremonial atmosphere that these kinds of songs helped to create. They were seldom heard, therefore, in family gatherings, at weddings, or at the dance. But where young people got together with their peers, perhaps over a can of beer from the canteen, the guitars and the mouth organs would come out, in a sort of casual way, and turn the bull session into a sing-song. So popular did this kind of music grow that when the Islanders returned from England, many more guitars found their way to Tristan.

It is fairly safe to predict that before long, the last trace of the old song tradition will have disappeared from Tristan da Cunha. In fact, the last solo in the old style may already have been sung — on New Year's Eve 1964 at the Administrator's house. Arthur Repetto seemed to be the last singer who was willing to perform such a solo in public, and apparently he was the last one who *could* do it without being exposed to smirks and teasing and even giggling laughter from the audience, particularly the younger people. And now, at the age of 66, Arthur has decided that England holds a better future for him and his family. He returned there in May 1966.

NOTES

1. For a brief survey of the history of Tristan da Cunha, see Peter A. Munch, *Sociology of Tristan da Cunha, Results of the Norwegian Scientific Expedition to Tristan da Cunha 1937-1938*, No. 13 (Oslo, 1945), pp. 13-47. A more detailed account of the history of the island is given by Jan Brander, *Tristan da Cunha, 1506-1902* (London, 1940).

2. Peter W. Green to the Admiralty, December 29, 1884: "Since 1870 we have had five shipwrecks on Tristan, two at Inaccessible, one at Gough's Island [250 miles south of Tristan], all a total loss. We received several ships' crews from ships abandoned at sea . . . " *Correspondence Relating to the Island of Tristan da Cunha* (London, 1887), p. 35. Hereafter cited as *Correspondence*.

3. Lindsay Brine, "Report upon the Island of Tristan d'Acunha," (November 1, 1876), *Correspondence*, p. 3; Munch, 1945, p. 39.

4. Day H. Bosanquet, "Report on the condition of the Inhabitants of Tristan da Cunha," (August 20, 1886), *Correspondence*, p. 55.

5. Munch, 1945, pp. 274-284.

6. These "appling days" or "egging days" were quite informal, with no sharp separation of work and play. The Tristan Islanders did not perform anything like the elaborate harvest festivals or other work celebrations, usually performed after the work is finished, which are so frequently found among "primitive" as well as "civilized" peoples.

7. See Alan Lomax, *The Folk Songs of North America in the English Language* (Garden City, N.Y., 1960), p. xix.

8. Munch, 1945, pp. 303-310.

9. According to Mrs. Barrow, who spent three years on Tristan as a minister's wife, 1906-1909, this tradition was believed to stem from Thomas Swain himself. He

"used to tell his children, of whom there were four daughters living on the island when we were there, that he was the sailor who caught Nelson when he fell at Trafalgar." K. M. Barrow, *Three Years in Tristan da Cunha* (London, 1910), p. 11.

10. William F. Taylor, *Some Account of the Settlement of Tristan d'Acunha, in the South Atlantic Ocean* (London, 1856), p. 35 f.

11. Munch, 1945, pp. 34 f., 45 ff., 241-248.

12. *Ibid.*, p. 211 ff. The "three brothers-in-law" whom Peter Green reported having lost in the lifeboat disaster of 1885 (along with his sons, grandsons, and a son-in-law) apparently were the two Swain brothers besides Thomas Glass, who was married to their sister. Peter Green to Colonial Office, November 28, 1885, *Correspondence*, p. 38.

13. Taylor, 1856, p. 16.

14. Augustus Earle, *A Narrative of Nine Months' Residence in New Zealand in 1827, Together with a Journal of a Residence in Tristan d'Acunha, an Island between South America and the Cape of Good Hope* (London, 1832), p. 309.

15. Through this marriage of her daughter to Peter Green, Sarah Williams eventually became the first ancestress of the whole community. The fact that all of the song transmitters in the Swain and Green kinship lines are descendants of the two sisters is not considered important in the present context as it is not known that these women carried a song tradition to Tristan da Cunha. Although both Maria Cotton and her niece, Mary Green, lived within the memory of the older people in 1938, they were never referred to as sources of island tradition.

16. Although it is not known that this band of sailors, Cotton, Swain, and Green, formed an outright opposition to William Glass, it is likely that the close relationships, particularly between the Cotton and Green families, laid the foundation for the rivalry that later developed between the Glass-Hagan coalition and the Cotton-Green-Repetto line of tradition. It may be significant that none of the numerous children of Alexander Cotton and Peter Green found a mate among William Glass's sixteen sons and daughters. In fact, there was never a marriage between a Glass and a Cotton, and the first marriage between a Glass and a Green took place in 1939.

17. The name of the sailor is not known. But the nickname he went by on Tristan was "Shorty."

18. The three Tristan versions are given on pages 51 f. For comparison, after each stanza of the Norwegian text, reference is made to the corresponding stanzas of the Tristan versions. The Norwegian text is from *Den første store viseboka,* edited by Egner, Gjelseth, Prøysen, and Siem (Oslo, n.d.), p. 139 f.

19. Taylor, 1856, p. 38.

20. Peter W. Green to the Admiralty, December 29, 1884, *Correspondence,* p. 34.

21. *Ibid.,* p. 35. We should possibly keep in mind that Peter Green always remained a sailor at heart, and that it was probably even more true then than it is today that sailors and whalers usually do not mix well. Besides, the American referred to in the passage was obviously Andrew Hagan, the captain of a whaling sloop who became a son-in-law of William Glass and Peter Green's most serious contestant for leadership on the island (see Munch, 1945, p. 34 f.).

22. Albert H. Tolman, "Some Songs Traditional in the United States," *Journal of American Folklore,* 29 (April - June 1916), 161 f.; MacEdward Leach, ed., *The Ballad Book* (New York, 1955), p. 278 f.

23. As usual, Child leaves an outsider to the finer points in balladry rather puzzled with regard to his criteria of authenticity; see Francis James Child, *The English and Scottish Popular Ballads* (Boston, 1882-1898), No. 84.

24. See, *e.g.,* Leach, 1955, p. 277.

25. Cecil J. Sharp, *English Folk Songs from the Southern Appalachians* (London, 1952, two volumes), I, 183-195.

26. Bertrand H. Bronson, *The Traditional Tunes of the Child Ballads* (Princeton, N.J., 1959-1966, three volumes), II, 325-391.

27. Eloise Hubbard Linscott, *Folk Songs of Old New England* (New York, 1939), p. 163 f.

28. In a previous publication (Peter A. Munch, "Traditional Songs of Tristan da Cunha," *Journal of American Folklore,* 74 [July-September 1961], 216 ff.), I have presented the Tristan version of "Barbara Allen" in 3/4 meter, but, on further reflection, consider this misleading, particularly since it may be construed to indicate a simple triple meter. Any conventional measure, of course, may be a straightjacket to an unaccompanied folk song, where "freedom combines with

simplicity to produce the characteristic rhythmical effects" (Bronson, I , 1959 , xxix).

29. Bronson, II (1963), 321.

30. The tune may be said to "lean to 5/4 time" in so far as this meter results if the long notes at every other stress are held just a little shorter. This may vary from one singer to the other and even from one performance to the other with the same singer, and since a long note, in actual folk singing, is seldom held exactly to the meter, the choice between a basic time of 3/2 or 5/4 in these versions of "Barbara Allen" may often be an arbitrary matter of notation.

31. Bronson, I (1959) x.

32. Arthur Palmer Hudson, *Folksongs of Mississippi and their Background* (Chapel Hill, 1936), p. 221.

33. For instance, Dailey Paskman and Sigmund Spaeth, *"Gentlemen, Be Seated!"* (Garden City, N.Y., 1928), p. 54 ff.

34. It should be noted that in the Tristan vernacular 'father' and 'farther' are undistinguishable, even to the Islanders themselves. This aspect of oral tradition is discussed in some detail by W. Edson Richmond, "Some Effects of Scribal and Typographical Error on Oral Tradition," *Southern Folklore Quarterly,* 15 (June 1951), 159-170, (reprinted in *The Critics & the Ballad,* eds. MacEdward Leach and Tristan P. Coffin [Carbondale, Ill., 1961] , pp. 225-235). Although his emphasis is on errors resulting from attempts to reduce oral tradition to writing, Richmond cites several examples from purely oral tradition of this "distortion complex" which results "from the unfamiliarity of . . . the singer of a song with the things which he utters and from the lack of any effective conservative force which makes exactness a virtue. Consequently, a tremendous amount of variation in oral literature may be explained in terms of the attempts which tale tellers, folk singers, and last — but far from least — editors and collectors of folkloristic materials have made, however unconsciously, to explain what they have heard in terms of what they *think* they have heard or in terms of what they know" (p. 160f.). Although phonetic memory is implied, Richmond seems to have overlooked its strong conservative effect.

35. In a previous publication of the song (Munch, 1961, p. 224 f.), the second word of the third line of stanza 2 was erroneously rendered as "foreman's." Since the Tristan dialect, again, would make little distinction between 'foreman' and 'foeman,' and since no recording equipment was available at the time the song was

written down, I could not now tell which word was used by the singer. Obviously, however, no matter what interpretation the singer gave the line, reference is to "our foeman's flagship."

36. "Bony Bay," or "Bony's Bay," appears to be a generic name for any French bay or harbor during the reign of Napoleon. The English used to refer to the French Emperor as "Bony" (for Bonaparte).

37. The account of the battle, as well as of the preceding events, including quotations, is from William Laird Clowes, *The Royal Navy: A History from the Earliest Times to the Present* (London, 1897-1903), IV, 351-372

38. Clowes, *op. cit.,* p. 365, note. — Several broadside ballads appear to have been in circulation praising the British victory in the battle of the Nile. Firth notes that "the two most popular ballads — to judge from the frequency of the reprints — were 'The Mouth of the Nile' and 'Battle of the Nile' " (C. H. Firth, *Naval Songs and Ballads,* printed for the Navy Records Society, 1908, p. xcv). A third ballad, "of which tradition has preserved merely a fragment" (p. xcvi), is published by Firth (p. 287). None of these appears to have any traditional relationship to "Little Powder-Monkey Jim."

39. Cf. Munch, 1945, pp. 63 f., 318 ff.

40. Cf. Robert Redfield, "The Folk Society," *The American Journal of Sociology,* 52 (January 1947), 296 f.

41. I would take exception to Bronson's statement that "the coefficient of change . . . is the level of intelligence of the folk-singing community and the liveliness of its artistic sensibility [sic];" Bertrand H. Bronson, "The Interdependence of Ballad Tunes and Texts," *California Folklore Quarterly,* 3 (July 1944), 205.

42. Lomax, 1960, p. xxvii.

43. Cf. Sharp, I (1952), xxxi.

44. *Ibid.,* xxix. Sharp is here probably referring not so much to the aesthetic qualities of the tune in an absolute sense as to the likelihood that such a tune would remain an independent piece of living folk tradition.

45. A discussion of this adaptation of the old British ballads is presented by

Tristram P. Coffin, *The British Traditional Ballad in North America*, rev. edn. (Philadelphia, 1963), p. 9 ff. Coffin is hardly right in assuming that the development of the old ballads "toward lyric" is particularly characteristic of the American variants.

46. The nostalgic attachment of some early ballad collectors and folklorists to what they conceived as "authentic" folk art and music contains in itself an element of romanticism and is a form of "cultured primitivism" which would be stuff for an interesting study in the sociology of knowledge that we shall not pursue here. Neither do I wish to enter into a discussion of the hair-splitting distinction between "folksong" (or "genuine folksong") and "popular song" except to say that from the point of view of the study of culture and cultural tradition, such a distinction seems to make little sense.

47. Leach, 1955, p. 698; cf. Lomax, 1960, p. 261ff.

48. Leach, 1955, p. 786 f.

49. See "The Gosport Tragedy" (Leach, 1955, p. 698 f.) and "Naomi Wise" or "Omie Wise" *(ibid.,* p. 793 ff.; Lomax, 1960, p. 268).

50. This is the scale, with the first and the fourth intervals increased, which is designated as π^4 in the system developed by Bertrand H. Bronson, "Folksong and the Modes," *The Musical Quarterly,* 32 (January 1946), 37 ff. (cf. Bronson, II (1963), xi ff). The scale is conventionally described as "lacking the 2nd and the 6th" and corresponds to Sharp's Mode 2 (1952, I, xxxii). Assuming that gap-fillers are most likely generated in singing simply by deflecting the higher tone of a large interval in a pentatonic scale, it appears that the heptatonic mode to which this pentatonic is most closely related is the Dorian, which has its semitone intervals immediately above the 2nd and the 6th. So it may conventionally be described as a pentatonic Dorian mode.

51. Lomax, 1960, p. 307.

52. William Main Doerflinger, *Shantymen and Shantyboys: Songs of the Sailor and Lumberman* (New York, 1951), p. 164.

53. This seems to be characteristic of the Anglo-American song tradition. Comparing the American Negro singer with the typical White bard, Lomax states (1960, p. xxvi): "If the Negro emphasis is on the improviser and his chorus, the white is upon the solo song rememberer and his silent audience. For the Negro, song is a natural part of life's activities; for the white a self-conscious moment of communication. . . ."

54. Cf. the development from "The Twa Corbies" and "The Three Rauens" to "The Three Crows" *(e.g.,* Leach, 1955, p. 111 ff.), or the reduction of "The Boyne Water," the ballad of the defeat of James II at the battle of the Boyne in 1690, to a mocking ditty in Pennsylvania or to a children's game song in Australia; for the texts from Pennsylvania and Australia see, respectively, George Korson, *Pennsylvania Songs and Legends* (Philadelphia, 1949), p. 48; Iona and Peter Opie, *The Lore and Language of Schoolchildren* (Oxford, 1959), p. 343.

55. This may indeed have been the case in some instances; but usually it was probably the other way around.

56. A purist in the study of folk dances may protest that most of the Tristan "waltzes" are not "real" waltzes at all, which, of course, is true. We are, however, concerned with the dance from a cultural point of view and are therefore primarily interested in the particular dance as a shared idea within the community rather than in what it "really" is according to criteria brought in from the outside.

57. This dance, identical in steps and tune, is still known in Maine.

58. No. 22A was whistled to me by Alfred Green himself when I visited his house to check some of my music notes made at a dance. But on his accordion he always gave the slightly more elaborate version, No. 22B.

59. The "swinging part" of No. 17 was referred to as the "alle-makte" (or "olle-mokte") part, but no one was able to furnish an explanation.

60. Robert Redfield, *Peasant Society and Culture* (Chicago, 1956), p. 70 ff. and *passim.*

61. Peter A. Munch, "Culture and Superculture in a Displaced Community: Tristan da Cunha," *Ethnology,* 3 (October 1964), 369-76.

62. D. M. Booy, *Rock of Exile: A Narrative of Tristan da Cunha* (London, 1957), p. 80 f.

63. Martin Holdgate, *Mountains in the Sea: The Story of the Gough Island Expedition* (London, 1958), p. 58 f.

64. Maud Karpeles, "A Report on Visits to the Tristan da Cunha Islanders," *Journal of the English Folk Dance and Song Society,* 9 (December 1962), 162 ff.

65. It was the same cast-away sailor who also introduced "Little Annie Rooney" to Tristan.

66. Roland Svensson, Swedish artist and writer, who has made a name for himself as an interpreter of island life in general, accompanied the Tristan Islanders on their way home as a passenger on the *Bornholm* (Roland Svensson, *Tristan da Cunha, South Atlantic* [Stockholm, 1965]. He made some tape recordings at one of the dances arranged on board, including the two songs presented by Arthur Repetto. Mr. Svensson very kindly allowed me during a subsequent visit to Stockholm to take copies of his valuable tapes. For this generosity I hereby express my most sincere thanks.

67. See above, p. 82 ff., cp. Karpeles, *op. cit.*, p. 166 f. The most conspicuous change is that the last note of the third line has been lengthened, thus bringing the tune into a regular triple meter throughout and eliminating the characteristic but irregular 9/8 bar at the end.

68. Unfortunately, the tape missed the first part of the first line.

69. In general, the texts of the Tristan songs were not strongly influenced by the pecularities of the Tristan vernacular. It is assumed that this was owing more than anything else, to phonetic memory and a deference to the form as transmitted rather than to a conscious desire to present the songs in "correct" English. However, as noted already in 1938 (see "The Old Miser," p. 79 f.), in Arthur Repetto's singing certain characteristics of Tristan speech came out clearly, such as the bilabial V which sounded almost like a W, the "intrusive R," and some difficulty with the past tense.

70. A similar version of the song, but not quite as mixed up, was obtained from Mary Swain in 1962 by Maud Karpeles *(op. cit.,* p. 165 f.).

LITERATURE CITED

Barrow, K.M. *Three Years in Tristan da Cunha.* London, 1910.

Booy, D.M. *Rock of Exile, A Narrative of Tristan da Cunha.* London, 1957.

Brander, Jan. *Tristan da Cunha, 1506-1902.* London, 1940.

Bronson, Bertrand H. "Folksong and the Modes," *The Musical Quarterly,* 32 (1946), 37 ff.

——. "The Interdependence of Ballad Tunes and Texts," *California Folklore Quarterly,* 3 (1944), 185-207; reprinted in MacEdward Leach and Tristram P. Coffin, eds., *The Critics and the Ballad,* Carbondale, 1961, pp. 77-102.

——. *The Traditional Tunes of the Child Ballads,* 3 vols., Princeton, N.J., 1959-1966.

Child, Francis James. *The English and Scottish Popular Ballads,* 5 vols., Boston, 1882-1898.

Clowes, Wm. Laird. *The Royal Navy, A History from the Earliest Times to the Present,* 7 vols., London, 1897-1903.

Coffin, Tristram P. *The British Traditional Ballad in North America,* Publications of the American Folklore Society, Bibliographical Series, vol. II, Philadelphia, 1950.

Correspondence Relating to the Island of Tristan d'Acunha, Presented to both Houses of Parliament by Command of Her Majesty, London, 1887.

Den første store viseboka (redaksjon: Egner, Gjelseth, Prøysen og Siem), Oslo, n.d.

Disher, Maurice Willson. *Victorian Song, From Dive to Drawing Room.* London, 1955.

Doerflinger, William Main. *Shantymen and Shantyboys, Songs of the Sailor and Lumberman.* New York, 1951.

Earle, Augustus. *A Narrative of Nine Months' Residence in New Zealand in 1827, Together with a Journal of a Residence in Tristan d'Acunha, an Island between South America and the Cape of Good Hope.* London, 1832.

Firth, C. H., ed. *Naval Songs and Ballads.* Printed for the Navy Records Society, 1908.

Greenleaf, Elisabeth Bristol. *Ballads and Sea Songs of Newfoundland.* Cambridge (Mass.), 1933.

Holdgate, Martin. *Mountains in the Sea, The Story of the Gough Island Expedition.* London, 1958.

Hudson, Arthur Palmer. *Folk Songs of Mississippi and their Background.* Chapel Hill, 1936.

Karpeles, Maud. "A Report on Visits to the Tristan da Cunha Islanders," *Journal of the English Folk Dance and Song Society,* 9 (1962), 162-167.

Korson, George. *Pennsylvania Songs and Legends.* Philadelphia, 1949.

Laws, G. Malcolm, Jr. *American Balladry from British Broadsides.* Publications of the American Folklore Society,   Bibliographical and Special Series, vol. VIII, Philadelphia, 1957.

——. *Native American Balladry.*   Publications of the American Folklore Society, Bibliographical and Special Series, vol. I, rev. edn., Philadelphia, 1964.

Leach, MacEdward, ed. *The Ballad Book.* New York, 1955.
——. and Tristram P. Coffin, eds. *The Critics and the Ballad.* Carbondale, 1961.

Linscott, Eloise Hubbard. *Folk Songs of Old New England.* New York, 1939.

Lomax, Alan. *Folk Song, U.S.A.* New York, 1947.

——. *The Folk Songs of North America in the English Language.* Garden City, N.Y., 1960.

Mackenzie, W. Roy. *Ballads and Sea Songs from Nova Scotia.* Hatboro, 1963.

Munch, Peter A. "Culture and Superculture in a Displaced Community, Tristan da Cunha," *Ethnology,* 3 (1964), 369-76.

——. *Sociology of Tristan da Cunha (Results of the Norwegian Scientific Expedition to Tristan da Cunha 1937-1938,* No. 13), Oslo, 1945.

——. "Traditional Songs of Tristan da Cunha," *Journal of American Folklore,* 74 (1961), 216-29.

Opie, Iona and Peter. *The Lore and Language of School Children.* Oxford, 1959.

Paskman, Dailey, and Sigmund Spaeth. *"Gentlemen, Be Seated!" A Parade of the Old-Time Minstrels.* Garden City, N.Y., 1928.

Redfield, Robert. "The Folk Society," *The American Journal of Sociology,* 52 (1946/47), 293-308.

——. *Peasant Society and Culture.* Chicago, 1956.

Richmond, W. Edson. "Some Effects of Scribal and Typographical Error on Oral Tradition," *Southern Folklore Quarterly,* 15 (1951), 159-170. Reprinted in MacEdward Leach and Tristram P. Coffin, *The Critics and The Ballad.* Carbondale, 1961, pp. 225-235.

Sharp, Cecil J. *English Folk Songs from the Southern Appalachians.* 2 impr., London, 1952.

Svensson, Roland. *Tristan da Cunha, South Atlantic.* Stockholm, 1965.

Taylor, William F. *Some Account of the Settlement of Tristan d'Acunha, in the South Atlantic Ocean.* London, 1856.

Tolman, Albert H. "Some Songs Traditional in the United States," *Journal of American Folklore,* 29 (1916), 155-197.

Wells, Evelyn Kendrick. *The Ballad Tree, A Study of British and American Ballads.* New York, 1950.

INDEX OF SONG TITLES AND FIRST LINES

References in italics indicate texts and tunes recorded on Tristan da Cunha.

INDEX OF NAMES